FIX-IT and FORGET-IT®
Favorite
SLOW COOKER RECIPES FOR MOM

150 Recipes Mom Will Love to Make, Eat, and Share!

HOPE COMERFORD

Photos by Bonnie Matthews

GoodBooks

New York, New York

Good Books books may be purchased in bulk at special discounts for sales promotion, corporate gifts, fund-raising, or educational purposes. Special editions can also be created to specifications. For details, contact the Special Sales Department, Good Books, 307 West 36th Street, 11th Floor, New York, NY 10018 or info@skyhorsepublishing.com.

Good Books is an imprint of Skyhorse Publishing, Inc.®, a Delaware corporation.

Visit our website at www.goodbooks.com.

10 9 8 7 6 5 4 3 2 1

Library of Congress Cataloging-in-Publication Data is available on file.

Cover design by Jane Sheppard
Cover photo by Bonnie Matthews

Print ISBN: 978-1-68099-288-5
Ebook ISBN: 978-1-68099-296-0

Printed in China

To my beautiful mother and Meme (grandma), who taught me to love cooking, and inspire me every day with their grace, determination, feistiness, gratitude, and abundance of love.

Table of Contents

Welcome to *Fix-It and Forget-It Favorite Slow Cooker Recipes for Mom* ❧ 1

Choosing a Slow Cooker ❧ 1

Slow Cooking Tips and Tricks and Other Things You May Not Know ❧ 4

Breakfast ❧ 7

Appetizers & Snacks ❧ 49

Soups, Stews & Chilies ❧ 91

Main Dishes ❧ 139

Side Dishes & Vegetables ❧ 227

Desserts ❧ 279

Metric Equivalent Measurements ❧ 320

Recipe and Ingredient Index ❧ 321

About the Author ❧ 333

Welcome to Fix-It and Forget-It Favorite Slow Cooker Recipes for Mom

We reached out to Team Fix-It and Forget-It and asked them for their favorite and most popular recipes for Mom. We ended up with 150 scrumptious and mom-approved dishes! Not only will moms love these recipes, but anyone Mom cooks for will love them too. The beauty of all these recipes is the "Fix-It and Forget-It" aspect of your marvelous slow cooker. It does all the work for you while you're at work, out shopping, taking a nap, sleeping at night, playing with the kids, visiting a friend, getting a mani-pedi, or wherever the day takes you! Let's face it; moms need easy. Put that slow cooker to work so you don't have to! Enjoy these incredible recipes, moms!

Choosing a Slow Cooker

Not all slow cookers are created equal . . . or work equally as well for everyone!

Those of us who use slow cookers frequently know we have our own preferences when it comes to which slow cooker we choose to use. For instance, I love my programmable slow cooker, but there are many programmable slow cookers I've tried that I've strongly disliked. Why? Because some go by increments of 15 or 30 minutes and some go by 4, 6, 8, or 10 hours. I dislike those restrictions, but I have family and friends who don't mind them at all! I am also pretty brand loyal when it comes to my manual slow cookers because I've had great success with those and have had unsuccessful moments with slow cookers of other brands.

So which slow cooker is best for your household? It really depends on how many people you're feeding and if you're going to be away from it for long periods of time. Here are my recommendations:

For a 2–3 person household	3–5-quart slow cooker
For a 4–5 person household	5–6-quart slow cooker
For a 6+ person household	6½–7-quart slow cooker

Large slow cooker advantages/disadvantages:

Advantages:
- You can fit a loaf pan or a baking dish into a 6- or 7-quart, depending on the shape of your cooker. That allows you to make bread or cakes, or even smaller quantities of main dishes. (Take your favorite baking dish and loaf pan along when you shop for a cooker to make sure they'll fit inside.)
- You can feed large groups of people or make larger quantities of food, allowing for leftovers or meals to freeze.

Disadvantages:
- They take up more storage room.
- They don't fit as neatly into a dishwasher.
- If your crock isn't ⅔–¾ full, you may burn your food.

Small slow cooker advantages/disadvantages:

Advantages:
- They're great for lots of appetizers, for serving hot drinks, for baking cakes straight in the crock, and for dorm rooms or apartments.
- They're a great option for making recipes of smaller quantities.

Disadvantages:
- Food in smaller quantities tends to cook more quickly than larger amounts. So keep an eye on it.
- Chances are, you won't have many leftovers. So, if you like to have leftovers, a smaller slow cooker may not be a good option for you.

My recommendation:

Have at least two slow cookers: one around 3 to 4 quarts and one 6 quarts or larger. A third would be a huge bonus (and a great advantage to your cooking repertoire!). The advantage of having at least a couple is you can make a larger variety of recipes. Also, you can make at least two or three dishes at once for a whole meal.

Manual vs. Programmable

If you are gone for only 6 to 8 hours a day, a manual slow cooker might be just fine for you. If you are gone for more than 8 hours during the day, I would highly recommend purchasing a programmable slow cooker that will switch to Warm when the cook time you set is up. It will allow you to cook a wider variety of recipes.

The two I use most frequently are my 4-quart manual slow cooker and my 6½-quart programmable slow cooker. I like that I can make smaller portions in my 4-quart slow cooker on days I don't need or want leftovers, but I also love how my 6½-quart slow cooker can accommodate whole chickens, turkey breasts, hams, or big batches of soups. I use them both often.

Get to Know Your Slow Cooker . . .

Plan a little time to get acquainted with your slow cooker. Each slow cooker has its own personality—just like your oven (and your car). Plus, many new slow cookers cook hotter and faster than earlier models. I think that with all of the concern for food safety, the slow-cooker manufacturers have amped up their settings so that High, Low, and Warm are all higher temperatures than in the older models. That means they cook hotter—and therefore faster—than the first slow cookers. The beauty of these little machines is that they're supposed to cook low and slow. We count on that when we flip the switch in the morning before we leave the house for 10 hours or so. So, because none of us knows what kind of temperament our slow cooker has until we try it out, nor how hot it cooks, don't assume anything. Save yourself some disappointment and make the first recipe in your new slow cooker on a day when you're at home. Cook it for the shortest amount of time the recipe calls for. Then, check the food to see if it's done. Or if you start smelling food that seems to be finished, turn off the cooker and rescue your food.

Also, all slow cookers seem to have a "hot spot," which is of great importance to know, especially when baking with your slow cooker. This spot may tend to burn food in that area if you're not careful. If you're baking directly in your slow cooker, I recommend covering the "hot spot" with some foil.

Take Notes . . .

Don't be afraid to make notes in your cookbook. It's yours! Chances are, it will eventually get passed down to someone in your family and they will love and appreciate all of your musings. Take note of which slow cooker you used and exactly how long it took to cook the recipe. The next time you make it, you won't need to try to remember. Apply what you learned to the next recipes you make in your cooker. If another recipe says it needs to cook 7–9 hours, and you've discovered your slow cooker cooks on the faster side, cook that recipe for 6–6½ hours and then check it. You can always cook a recipe longer—but you can't reverse things if it's overdone.

Get Creative . . .

If you know your morning is going to be hectic, prepare everything the night before, take it out so the crock warms up to room temperature when you first get up in the morning, and then plug it in and turn it on as you're leaving the house.

 If you want to make something that has a short cook time and you're going to be gone longer than that, cook it the night before and refrigerate it for the next day. Warm it up when you get home. Or cook those recipes on the weekend when you know you'll be home and eat them later in the week.

Slow Cooking Tips and Tricks and Other Things You May Not Know

- Slow cookers tend to work best when they're ²/₃ to ¾ of the way full. You may need to increase the cooking time if you've exceeded that amount, or reduce it if you've put in less than that. If you're going to exceed that limit, it would be best to reduce the recipe, or split it between two slow cookers. (Remember how I suggested owning at least two or three slow cookers?)
- Keep your veggies on the bottom. That puts them in more direct contact with the heat. The fuller your slow cooker, the longer it will take its contents to cook. Also, the more densely packed the cooker's contents are, the longer they will take to cook. And finally, the larger the chunks of meat or vegetables, the more time they will need to cook.
- Keep the lid on! Every time you take a peek, you lose 20 minutes of cooking time. Please take this into consideration each time you lift the lid! I know, some of you can't help yourself and are going to lift anyway. Just don't forget to tack on 20 minutes to your cook time for each time you peeked!
- Sometimes it's beneficial to remove the lid. If you'd like your dish to thicken a bit, take the lid off during the last half hour to hour of cooking time.
- If you have a big slow cooker (7- to 8-quart), you can cook a small batch in it by putting the recipe ingredients into an oven-safe baking dish or baking pan and then placing that into the cooker's crock. First, put a trivet or some metal jar rings on the bottom of the crock, and then set your dish or pan on top of them. Or a loaf pan may "hook onto" the top ridges of the crock belonging to a large oval cooker and hang there straight and securely, "baking" a cake or quick bread. Cover the cooker and flip it on.

- The outside of your slow cooker will be hot! Please remember to keep it out of reach of children and keep that in mind for yourself as well!
- Get yourself a quick-read meat thermometer and use it! This helps remove the question of whether or not your meat is fully cooked, and helps prevent you from overcooking your meat as well.

Internal cooking temperatures:
  - Beef—125°F–130°F (rare); 140°F–145°F (medium); 160°F (well-done)
  - Pork—140°F–145°F (rare); 145°F–150°F (medium); 160°F (well-done)
  - Turkey and chicken—165°F

- Frozen meat: The basic rule of thumb is don't put frozen meat into the slow cooker. The meat does not reach the proper internal temperature in time. This especially applies to thick cuts of meat. Proceed with caution!
- Add fresh herbs 10 minutes before the end of the cooking time to maximize their flavor.
- If your recipe calls for cooked pasta, add it 10 minutes before the end of the cooking time if the cooker is on High, or 30 minutes before the end of the cooking time if it's on Low. Then the pasta won't get mushy.
- If your recipe calls for sour cream or cream, stir it in 5 minutes before the end of the cooking time. You want it to heat but not boil or simmer.

Approximate slow cooker temperatures (remember, each slow cooker is different):
  - High—212°F–300°F
  - Low—170°F–200°F
  - Simmer—185°F
  - Warm—165°F

Cooked and dried bean measurements: :
  - 16-oz. can, drained = about 1¾ cups beans
  - 19-oz. can, drained = about 2 cups beans
  - 1 lb. dried beans (about 2½ cups) = 5 cups cooked beans

Breakfast

Chunky Applesauce

Colleen Heatwole, Burton, MI

Makes 8 servings
Prep. Time: 20 minutes ♣ Cooking Time: 6 hours ♣ Ideal slow-cooker size: 5½-qt.

10 large cooking apples such as Granny Smith, Fuji, Braeburn, or Jonagold

½ cup water

1 tsp. cinnamon

⅓ to ¾ cup sugar, to taste

1. Peel, core, and chop apples.

2. Combine apples with the rest of the ingredients in slow cooker. Start with the lesser amount of sugar and taste again at the end.

3. Cover and cook on Low for 6 hours. Serve warm.

Almond Date Oatmeal

Audrey L. Kneer, Williamsfield, IL

Makes 8 servings
Prep. Time: 5 minutes   ♣   *Cooking Time: 4–8 hours, or overnight*   ♣   *Ideal slow-cooker size: 3-qt.*

2 cups rolled oats
½ cup Grape Nuts cereal
½ cup chopped almonds
¼ cup chopped dates
4½ cups water

1. Combine all ingredients in slow cooker.

2. Cover and cook on Low 4–8 hours, or overnight.

3. Serve with fat-free milk.

Pineapple Baked Oatmeal

Sandra Haverstraw, Hummelstown, PA

Makes 5–6 servings

Prep. Time: 5 minutes 🔹 Cooking Time: 1½–2½ hours 🔹 Ideal slow-cooker size: 2- to 3½-qt.

1 box of 8 instant oatmeal packets, any flavor

1½ tsp. baking powder

2 eggs, beaten

½ cup milk

8-oz. can crushed pineapple in juice, undrained

1. Spray inside of slow cooker with nonstick spray.

2. Empty packets of oatmeal into a large bowl. Add baking powder and mix.

3. Stir in eggs, milk, and undrained pineapple. Mix well. Pour mixture into slow cooker.

4. Cover and cook on High 1½ hours, or on Low 2½ hours.

TIPS

1. Serve warm as is, or with milk, for breakfast.

2. This is also a good, hearty, not-too-sweet dessert served with ice cream.

3. Individual servings reheat well in the microwave for a quick breakfast.

Apple Cinnamon Oatmeal

Hope Comerford, Clinton Township, MI

Makes 2–3 servings
Prep. Time: 5 minutes   &   Cooking Time: 7 hours   &   Ideal slow-cooker size: 2-qt.

½ cup steel cut oats
2 cups sweetened vanilla almond milk
1 small apple, peeled and diced
¼ tsp. cinnamon

1. Spray crock with nonstick spray.

2. Place all ingredients into crock and stir lightly.

3. Cover and cook on Low for 7 hours.

German Chocolate Oatmeal

Hope Comerford, Clinton Township, MI

Makes 4 servings
Prep. Time: 5 minutes   ❧   Cooking Time: 6–8 hours   ❧   Ideal slow-cooker size: 3-qt.

2 cups steel cut oats

8 cups unsweetened coconut milk

¼ cup unsweetened cocoa powder

¼ tsp. kosher salt

Brown sugar, to taste

Sweetened shredded coconut, to taste

1. Spray crock with nonstick spray.

2. Place steel cut oats, coconut milk, cocoa powder, and salt into crock and stir to mix.

3. Cover and cook on Low for 6–8 hours.

4. To serve, top each bowl of oatmeal with desired amount of brown sugar and shredded coconut.

Slow Cooker Maple and Brown Sugar Oatmeal

Jessica Stoner, Plain City, OH

Makes 4–6 servings

Prep. Time: 15–20 minutes ⚬ *Cooking Time: 2–6 hours* ⚬ *Ideal slow-cooker size: 4-qt.*

2 Tbsp. real maple syrup

2 Tbsp. flaxseed, *optional*

1 cup steel cut oats

3 Tbsp. brown sugar

½–1 cup raisins

½–1 cup Craisins

1½ cups milk

1½ cups water

1 tsp. cinnamon

1 Tbsp. butter

1. Spray crock with nonstick cooking spray.

2. Add all ingredients to slow cooker.

3. Cover and cook on Low for 5–6 hours, or 2–3 hours on High.

Serving suggestion:
For a little extra "crunch,"
add some sliced almonds.

Apple Breakfast Risotto

Hope Comerford, Clinton Township, MI

Makes 4 servings
Prep. Time: 10 minutes ❧ Cooking Time: 8 hours ❧ Ideal slow-cooker size: 3-qt.

4 Granny Smith apples, peeled and sliced

2 cups apple juice

2 cups water

2½ cups Arborio rice

¼ cup brown sugar

1½ tsp. cinnamon

¼ tsp. salt

1 tsp. vanilla extract

⅛ tsp. cloves

⅛ tsp. nutmeg

4 Tbsp. butter, sliced

1. Spray crock with nonstick spray.

2. Place all ingredients into crock and stir.

3. Cover and cook on Low for 8 hours.

Breakfast Apples

Joyce Bowman, Lady Lake, FL ❧ *Jeanette Oberholtzer, Manheim, PA*

Makes 4 servings
Prep. Time: 10–15 minutes ❧ *Cooking Time: 2–8 hours* ❧ *Ideal slow-cooker size: 3-qt.*

4 medium-sized apples, peeled and sliced

¼ cup honey

1 tsp. cinnamon

2 Tbsp. melted butter

2 cups dry granola cereal

1. Place apples in your slow cooker.

2. Combine remaining ingredients. Sprinkle the mixture evenly over top of the apples.

3. Cover and cook on Low 6–8 hours or overnight, or on High 2–3 hours.

Serving suggestion:

Serve as a side dish to bacon and bagels, or use as a topping for waffles, French toast, pancakes, or cooked oatmeal.

Fresh Veggie and Herb Omelet

Hope Comerford, Clinton Township, MI

Makes 8 servings
Prep. Time: 20 minutes ❧ Cooking Time: 4–6 hours ❧ Ideal slow-cooker size: 6-qt.

12 eggs
1 cup unsweetened almond milk or milk
½ tsp. kosher salt
¼ tsp. pepper
3 cloves garlic, minced
1 tsp. fresh chopped basil
6 dashes hot sauce
2 cups broccoli florets
1 yellow bell pepper, diced
1 red bell pepper, diced
1 onion, diced
1 cup crumbled feta cheese
1 cup diced cherry tomatoes
½ cup fresh chopped parsley

1. Spray crock with nonstick spray.

2. In a bowl, mix together eggs, milk, salt, pepper, garlic, basil, and hot sauce.

3. Place broccoli, yellow pepper, red pepper, and onion in crock. Gently mix with a spoon.

4. Pour egg mixture over the top.

5. Cover and cook on Low for 4–6 hours, or until center is set.

6. Sprinkle feta over the top, then cook an additional 30 minutes.

7. To serve, sprinkle the omelet with the chopped tomatoes and fresh parsley.

Kelly's Company Omelet

Kelly Bailey, Dillsburg, PA

Makes 12 servings
Prep. Time: 15 minutes ♣ *Cooking Time: 7–9 hours* ♣ *Ideal slow-cooker size: 6-qt.*

32-oz. bag frozen hash brown potatoes, or 5 cups cooked, shredded potatoes

1 lb. ham, bacon, or sausage, cooked and chopped

1 onion, chopped

1 green bell pepper, chopped

1 cup sliced fresh mushrooms

2 cups shredded cheddar cheese

12 eggs

1 cup whole milk

1 Tbsp. thyme, basil, rosemary, or tarragon, depending on what you like

½ tsp. cayenne pepper

1. In lightly greased slow cooker, place ⅓ of potatoes, ⅓ of ham, ⅓ of onion, ⅓ of green pepper, ⅓ of mushrooms, and ⅓ of cheese.

2. Repeat layers twice, ending with cheese.

3. In a mixing bowl, whisk together eggs, milk, the herb you chose, and cayenne.

4. Pour egg mixture gently over the layers in the slow cooker.

5. Cover and cook on Low 7–9 hours, until omelet is set in the middle and lightly browned at edges.

Cheese Strata

Hope Comerford, Clinton Township, MI

Makes 6 servings
Prep. Time: 10 minutes ❧ Cooking Time: 4–6 hours ❧ Ideal slow-cooker size: 3-qt.

14 slices of bread, cut up or torn into bite-sized pieces

4 Tbsp. butter, cut into approximately 8 pieces

3 cups shredded sharp cheddar cheese, *divided*

6 large eggs

3 cups milk, warmed for 3 minutes in the microwave

1 small onion, chopped finely

2 Tbsp. Worcestershire sauce

3–4 dashes hot sauce

1 tsp. garlic powder

1 tsp. onion powder

Salt and pepper, to taste

1. Spray your crock well with nonstick spray.

2. Place half the bread in bottom of crock. Place 4 pieces of butter on top of bread. Spread 1½ cups of shredded cheese on top of that. Repeat this process with remaining bread, butter, and cheese.

3. Mix eggs, milk, onion, Worcestershire sauce, hot sauce, garlic powder, onion powder, salt, and pepper together. Pour this mixture over bread and cheese layers.

4. Cover and cook on Low for 4–6 hours.

Zucchini Quiche

Anita Troyer, Fairview, MI

Makes 6 servings
Prep. Time: 20 minutes ⚘ Cooking Time: 3 hours ⚘ Ideal slow-cooker size: 4-qt.

3–4 cups grated zucchini
4 eggs, beaten
¼ cup vegetable oil
¾ cup Bisquick
¾ tsp. salt
¼ tsp. garlic powder
½ cup grated cheese
1 tsp. dried oregano
Pinch of dried basil

1. Mix together all ingredients in given order. Pour into a greased slow cooker.

2. Cover and cook on High for 3 hours.

"Hash Brown" Cauliflower Breakfast Bake

Hope Comerford, Clinton Township, MI

Makes 8–10 servings

Prep. Time: 20 minutes ❧ Cooking Time: 7 hours ❧ Ideal slow-cooker size: 6-qt.

12 eggs

½ cup unsweetened almond milk or milk

1 tsp. kosher salt

1 tsp. garlic powder

1 tsp. onion powder

¼ tsp. pepper

1 head cauliflower, shredded

1 medium onion, chopped

1 lb. turkey sausage, browned and drained

2 cups shredded cheddar cheese, *divided*

1. In a bowl, mix together eggs, milk, salt, garlic powder, onion powder, and pepper.

2. Spray crock with nonstick spray.

3. Combine cauliflower, onion, and turkey sausage in a bowl.

4. Spread ⅓ of the cauliflower mixture into bottom of crock. Top this with ⅓ of egg mixture, then top with ⅓ of cheese. Repeat this process 2 more times.

5. Cover and cook on Low for 7 hours.

Blueberry Fancy

Leticia A. Zehr, Lowville, NY

Makes 12 servings
Prep. Time: 10–15 minutes ❧ *Cooking Time: 3–4 hours* ❧ *Ideal slow-cooker size: 5-qt.*

I loaf Italian bread, cubed, *divided*
I pint blueberries, *divided*
8 ozs. cream cheese, cubed, *divided*
6 eggs
1½ cups milk

1. Place half the bread cubes in the slow cooker.

2. Drop half the blueberries over top of the bread.

3. Sprinkle half the cream cheese cubes over blueberries.

4. Repeat all 3 layers.

5. In a mixing bowl, whisk together eggs and milk. Pour over all ingredients in crock.

6. Cover and cook on Low until the dish is custardy and set.

Serving suggestion:

Serve with maple syrup or blueberry sauce.

French Toast

Janie Steele, Moore, OK

Makes 6–8 servings
Prep. Time: 30 minutes ⚜ Refrigeration Time: 4 hours, or overnight ⚜ Cooking Time: 1½–3 hours ⚜
Ideal slow-cooker size: 5-qt.

1 loaf crusty, cubed
(older bread works best)

2 Tbsp. unsalted butter

3 Tbsp. brown sugar

1 cup chopped pecans

4 eggs

2 cups half-and-half

1 Tbsp. vanilla extract

1 tsp. cinnamon

¼ tsp. nutmeg

¼ tsp. salt

Caramel sauce, store-bought

1. Grease slow cooker.

2. Add bread cubes to crock.

3. Combine butter and brown sugar. Mix to consistency of pebbles, then add pecans. Set aside.

4. Whisk eggs, half-and-half, vanilla, cinnamon, nutmeg, and salt together in a bowl. Pour mixture over bread and mix to saturate.

5. Cover and refrigerate at least 4 hours or overnight.

6. Take crock out of refrigerator and let crock warm up a bit. Sprinkle butter mixture evenly over the saturated bread cubes.

7. Cook on Low for 3 hours or High for 1½ hours, or until bubbly and bread is brown.

8. Serve on plates with caramel sauce drizzled over top. Serve hot.

Serving suggestion:
Serve with breakfast meat or fresh fruit on the side.

French Toast Casserole

Michele Ruvola, Vestal, NY

Makes 9 servings

Prep. Time: 30 minutes ⚬ *Cooking Time: 2–4 hours* ⚬ *Ideal slow-cooker size: 5- to 6½-qt.*

2 eggs

2 egg whites

1½ cups milk, preferably 2%

5 Tbsp. honey, *divided*

1 tsp. vanilla extract

2 tsp. cinnamon, *divided*

3 cups finely diced apple

⅓ cup chopped, toasted pecans

1 tsp. lemon juice

9 slices bread of your choice

1. In a mixing bowl, whisk together eggs, egg whites, milk, 2 Tbsp. honey, vanilla, and 1 tsp. cinnamon.

2. Separately, remaining 3 Tbsp. honey, remaining 1 tsp. cinnamon, combine apple, pecans, and lemon juice. Set aside.

3. In a greased slow cooker, place one layer of bread, cutting to fit (triangles are good).

4. Layer in ¼ of the apple filling. Repeat layers, making 3 layers of bread and 4 of filling, ending with filling on top.

5. Pour egg mixture gently over everything.

6. Cover and cook on High 2–2½ hours or on Low 4 hours, or until bread has soaked up the liquid and apples are soft.

Serving suggestion:
Serve with warm maple syrup.

Caramel Rolls

Jessalyn Wantland, Paris, TX

Makes 6–8 servings
Prep. Time: 20 minutes ❧ Cooking Time: 2–3 hours ❧ Ideal slow-cooker size: 5-qt.

½ cup brown sugar
½ tsp. cinnamon
4 Tbsp. (½ stick) butter
2 8-oz. pkgs. refrigerator biscuits

1. Mix sugar and cinnamon together in a small bowl.

2. Melt butter in another small bowl.

3. Dip individual biscuits into melted butter and then into cinnamon and sugar mixture.

4. Place each covered biscuit in a greased slow cooker.

5. Cover and cook on High for 2–3 hours, or until rolls are done. Check rolls in center after 2 hours to see if they are done.

Custard Cinnamon Rolls

Sue Hamilton, Benson, AZ

Makes 8 servings
Prep. Time: 5 minutes & Cooking Time: 2 hours & Ideal slow-cooker size: 4-qt.

3½ cups full-fat vanilla ice cream
(half a 1¾-quart box)

8 refrigerator cinnamon rolls with icing

1. Turn slow cooker on High to preheat.

2. Place ice cream in crock, flattening it out as the ice cream softens.

3. Press cinnamon rolls into ice cream.

4. Cover and cook on High for 2 hours, or until the ice cream is a thick custard and the rolls are baked through.

5. Serve a roll with custard, and top with icing.

Poppy Seed Tea Bread

Julie Hurst, Leola, PA

Makes 10 servings
Prep. Time: 30 minutes ❧ Cooking Time: 3–4 hours ❧ Standing Time: 30 minutes ❧
Ideal slow-cooker size: 6-qt.

½ cup whole wheat flour

1½ cups all-purpose flour

¾ cup sugar

2 tsp. baking powder

¼ tsp. salt

¼ cup poppy seeds

2 eggs, at room temperature

8 Tbsp. (1 stick) salted butter, melted

¾ cup whole milk, at room temperature

½ tsp. almond extract

½ tsp. vanilla extract

1. In a mixing bowl, combine flours, sugar, baking powder, salt, and poppy seeds.

2. Separately, whisk together eggs, butter, milk, and extracts.

3. Pour wet ingredients into flour mixture, stirring until just combined.

4. Make sure your loaf pan fits in your oval 6-quart slow cooker. Grease and flour loaf pan. Set it on a jar ring or other heat-resistant item to keep it off the floor of the cooker.

5. Pour batter into prepared loaf pan.

6. Put lid on cooker, propping it open at one end with a chopstick or wooden spoon handle.

7. Cook on High for 3–4 hours, until a tester inserted in middle comes out clean.

8. Wearing oven mitts (to protect your knuckles!), remove hot pan from hot cooker and allow it to cool for 10 minutes. Run a knife around the edge and turn loaf out on a cooling rack to cool for an additional 20 minutes before slicing.

Raspberry Chocolate Chip Bread

Rosanna Martin, Morgantown, WV

Makes 10 servings
Prep. Time: 25 minutes ☙ Cooking Time: 3–4 hours ☙ Ideal slow-cooker size: 6-qt.

1 cup whole wheat flour
⅔ cup all-purpose flour
¾ cup rolled oats
⅔ cup sugar
2 tsp. baking powder
1 tsp. baking soda
½ tsp. salt
½ tsp. cinnamon
¾ cup fresh or unsweetened frozen raspberries (do not thaw)
⅔ cup chocolate chips
1 egg, lightly beaten
¾ cup buttermilk
⅓ cup canola oil
1 tsp. vanilla extract

1. In a large bowl, mix flours, oats, sugar, baking powder, baking soda, salt, and cinnamon. Gently stir in raspberries and chocolate chips.

2. Separately, mix egg, buttermilk, oil, and vanilla.

3. Gently stir wet ingredients into dry until just barely mixed—streaks of flour are fine.

4. Make sure your loaf pan fits in your oval 6-quart slow cooker. Grease and flour loaf pan. Set it on a jar ring or other heat-resistant item to keep it off the floor of the cooker.

5. Pour batter into prepared loaf pan.

6. Put lid on cooker, propping it open at one end with a chopstick or wooden spoon handle.

7. Cook on High for 3–4 hours, until a tester inserted in middle comes out clean.

8. Wearing oven mitts (to protect your knuckles!), remove hot pan from hot cooker and allow it to cool for 10 minutes. Run a knife around the edge and turn loaf out on a cooling rack to cool for an additional 30 minutes before slicing.

Appetizers & Snacks

Angie's Cheese Dip

Colleen Heatwole, Burton, MI

Makes 6–8 servings
Prep. Time: 5 minutes & Cooking Time: 2 hours & Ideal slow-cooker size: 2-qt.

8 ozs. sharp cheddar cheese, cubed

15-oz. can or jar of cheddar cheese sauce

15-oz. can chili with or without beans

1. Combine all ingredients in slow cooker.

2. Heat on Low until cheese melts, stirring occasionally.

3. Stir before serving.

Serving suggestion:

Serve with tortilla chips and/or crackers of choice.

Lori's Two-Ingredient Cheese Sauce

Colleen Heatwole, Burton, MI

Makes 1–6 servings

Prep. Time: 5 minutes ⚬ *Cooking Time: 2 hours* ⚬ *Ideal slow-cooker size: 2-qt.*

8 ozs. cream cheese, softened

15-oz. can chili with beans

1. Cube softened cream cheese into 8 pieces.

2. Add cream cheese to greased slow cooker.

3. Add chili with beans.

4. Cover. Cook on Low 2 hours, stirring occasionally.

Serving suggestion:

Serve with tortilla chips and/or crackers of choice.

Bacon Cheddar Dip

Arlene Snyder, Millerstown, PA

Makes 15 servings
Prep. Time: 10–15 minutes   ℐ   Cooking Time: 1½–2 hours   ℐ   Ideal slow-cooker size: 4-qt.

2 8-oz. pkgs. cream cheese, softened

2 cups sour cream

1 lb. bacon, fried and crumbled

4 cups shredded cheddar cheese, *divided*

1. In a mixing bowl, beat cream cheese and sour cream until smooth.

2. Fold in bacon and 3 cups cheddar cheese.

3. Place mixture in slow cooker and sprinkle with remaining cheese.

4. Cover and cook on Low 1½–2 hours, or until heated through.

Serving suggestion:

Serve with white corn chips.

TIPS

1. Save a few bacon crumbles to sprinkle on top.

2. For a spicier version, stir in some fresh herbs or some chopped chilies in Step 2.

Crab Spread

Jeanette Oberholtzer, Manheim, PA

Makes 8 servings

Prep. Time: 20 minutes 🔸 Cooking Time: 4 hours 🔸 Ideal slow-cooker size: 1- to 3-qt.

½ cup mayonnaise

8 ozs. cream cheese, softened

2 Tbsp. apple juice

1 onion, minced

1 lb. lump crabmeat, picked over to remove cartilage and shell bits

1. Mix mayonnaise, cheese, and juice in a medium-sized bowl until blended.

2. Stir in onion, mixing well. Gently stir in crabmeat.

3. Place in slow cooker, cover, and cook on Low for 4 hours.

4. Dip will hold for 2 hours. Stir occasionally.

Serving suggestion:

Serve with snack crackers, snack bread, or crudités.

Roasted Pepper and Artichoke Spread

Sherril Bieberly, Sauna, KS

Makes 3 cups, or about 12 servings
Prep. Time: 10 minutes ❧ Cooking Time: 1 hour ❧ Ideal slow-cooker size: 1- to 1½-qt.

1 cup grated Parmesan cheese
½ cup mayonnaise
8 ozs. cream cheese, softened
1 clove garlic, minced
14-oz. can artichoke hearts, drained and chopped finely
⅓ cup finely chopped roasted red bell peppers (from 7¼-oz. jar)

1. Combine Parmesan cheese, mayonnaise, cream cheese, and garlic in food processor. Process until smooth. Place mixture in slow cooker.

2. Add artichoke hearts and roasted peppers. Stir well.

3. Cover. Cook on Low 1 hour. Stir again.

Serving suggestion:
Serve as a spread for crackers, with cut-up fresh vegetables, or on bread slices.

Garlicky Spinach Artichoke Dip

Hope Comerford, Clinton Township, MI

Makes 6–8 servings
Prep. Time: 10 minutes ⚜ Cooking Time: 4 hours ⚜ Ideal slow-cooker size: 3-qt.

9 ozs. frozen chopped spinach, thawed and drained

14-oz. can quartered artichoke hearts, drained

½ cup plain nonfat Greek yogurt

4 ozs. reduced-fat cream cheese, at room temperature

8 cloves garlic, minced

1 cup shredded mozzarella cheese

½ cup shredded Parmesan cheese

¼ tsp. pepper

½ tsp. kosher salt

1. Spray crock with nonstick spray.

2. Place all ingredients into crock and stir to combine well.

3. Cover and cook on Low for 4 hours.

Serving suggestion:

Serve with tortilla chips, pita chips, or pumpernickel bread.

Slim Dunk

Vera Smucker, Goshen, IN

Makes 3 cups, or 12 servings
Prep. Time: 20 minutes & Cooking Time: 1 hour & Ideal slow-cooker size: 1½-qt.

2 cups fat-free sour cream

¼ cup fat-free Miracle Whip salad dressing

10 ozs. frozen chopped spinach, thawed and squeezed dry

1.8-oz. envelope dry leek soup mix

¼ cup minced red bell pepper

1. Combine all ingredients in slow cooker. Mix well.

2. Cover and cook on High for 1 hour.

Serving suggestion:
Serve with baked tortilla chips.

French Onion Dip

Hope Comerford, Clinton Township, MI

Makes 6 servings
Prep. Time: 10 minutes & Cooking Time: 8 hours & Ideal slow-cooker size: 2-qt.

2 large sweet yellow onions, finely chopped

4 Tbsp. olive oil

1 ½ cups plain nonfat Greek yogurt

2 cloves garlic, minced

2 tsp. Worcestershire sauce

¼ tsp. salt

¼ tsp. pepper

Pinch of cayenne

1. Place onions and olive oil in the crock and stir so onions are coated in the olive oil.

2. Cover and cook on Low for 8 hours, or until the onions are a deep caramel brown color.

3. Strain the onions.

4. In a bowl, combine yogurt, garlic, Worcestershire sauce, salt, pepper, cayenne, and onions.

Serving suggestion:

Serve with potato chips.

Green Olive Bean Dip

Hope Comerford, Clinton Township, MI

Makes 30 servings
Prep. Time: 15 minutes 🌣 Cooking Time: 3 hours 🌣 Ideal slow-cooker size: 3-qt.

16-oz. can nonfat refried beans

2 cups salsa of your choice

1 small onion, chopped

2 Tbsp. chili powder

1 tsp. onion powder

3 cloves garlic, minced

3 cups shredded mozzarella cheese

5¾-oz. jar sliced green olives with pimentos, drained

Tortilla chips for serving

1. In the crock, mix together all of the ingredients.

2. Cover and cook on Low for 3 hours. Stir occasionally.

Serving suggestion:

Serve with tortilla chips.

Pesto Tomato Spread

Nanci Keatley, Salem, OR

Makes 12 servings
Prep. Time: 20 minutes & Cooking Time: 2–3 hours & Ideal slow-cooker size: 2-qt.

2 8-oz. pkgs. cream cheese, at room temperature

⅔ cup prepared pesto

3 tomatoes, chopped

½ cup sliced black olives

½ cup chopped fresh basil

1 cup shredded mozzarella

½ cup grated Parmesan cheese

1. Place cream cheese in bottom of lightly greased slow cooker. Push gently to make an even layer.

2. Layer rest of ingredients on top in order given.

3. Cover and cook on Low for 2–3 hours, until cheese is melted and spread is hot throughout.

Serving suggestion:

Serve as a spread on crackers or thin slices of Italian bread or toast.

Herbed Cheese Terrine

Nancy J. Reppert, Mechanicsburg, PA

Makes 20 servings

Prep. Time: 20 minutes ❧ Cooking Time: 3–5 hours ❧ Chilling Time: 9 hours ❧ Ideal slow-cooker size: 6-qt.

2 8-oz. pkgs. cream cheese, at room temperature

½ cup crumbled feta cheese

½ tsp. garlic powder

⅛ tsp. pepper

½ cup plain Greek yogurt

2 eggs

2 tsp. finely grated lemon peel

½ cup chopped fresh herbs (any combination of parsley, basil, cilantro, or dill)

2 green onions, thinly sliced

¼ cup minced sun-dried tomatoes (drained if oil-packed)

¼ cup chopped Greek black olives

Red and green lettuce leaves, for serving

Crackers or baguette slices, for serving

1. In a mixing bowl, beat cream cheese. Add feta, garlic powder, and pepper and beat again.

2. Mix in yogurt, eggs, and lemon peel until just smooth again.

3. Stir in herbs, onions, tomatoes, and olives.

4. Pour water into slow cooker to a depth of 1–2 inches.

5. Prepare an 8-inch loaf pan by greasing it well and placing a rectangle of parchment paper on its bottom. Pour cheese mixture into prepared pan.

6. Lower pan into water in cooker—the water should come up about halfway on the pan.

7. Cover and cook on High for 3–5 hours, until center of loaf is softly set.

8. Wearing oven mitts to protect your knuckles, remove hot pan from cooker and allow to cool for 1 hour. Cover and chill for at least 8 hours.

9. Gently unmold terrine on a bed of lettuce leaves on a platter. Serve with crackers or baguette slices.

Colorful Fruit Salsa

Joyce Shackelford, Green Bay, WI

Makes 8–10 servings
Prep. Time: 25 minutes ❧ Cooking Time: 2 hours ❧ Ideal slow-cooker size: 3-qt.

11-oz. can mandarin oranges

8½-oz. can sliced peaches in juice, undrained

8-oz. can pineapple tidbits in juice, undrained

1 medium onion, chopped finely

½ cup finely chopped green bell pepper

½ cup finely chopped red bell pepper

1 jalapeño pepper, chopped finely

3 cloves garlic, minced

3 Tbsp. cornstarch

1 tsp. salt

Juice of 1 lime

Zest of 1 lime, cut in fine strips (not finely grated)

¼ cup chopped fresh cilantro

Tortilla chips, for serving

1. Combine fruits, onion, peppers, garlic, cornstarch, and salt in slow cooker.

2. Cover and cook on High for 2 hours, stirring once each hour. Salsa should be thick and steaming, with the peppers softened.

3. Add lime juice and zest. Add cilantro. Remove salsa from slow cooker to a serving dish. Allow to cool for about 15 minutes before serving with tortilla chips.

Peach Chutney

Jan Mast, Lancaster, PA

Makes 8 cups
Prep. Time: 10 minutes & Cooking Time: 5–8 hours & Ideal slow-cooker size: 4-qt.

2 29-oz. cans (about 6 cups) peaches, diced
1 cup raisins
1 small onion, chopped
1 clove garlic, minced
1 Tbsp. mustard seed
1 tsp. chopped dried red chilies
¼ cup chopped crystallized ginger
1 tsp. salt
¾ cup vinegar
½ cup brown sugar

1. Combine all ingredients in slow cooker.

2. Cover. Cook on Low 4–6 hours.

3. Remove lid. Stir chutney. Cook on High, uncovered, an additional 1–2 hours.

Apple-y Kielbasa

Jeanette Oberholtzer, Manheim, PA

Makes 12 servings

Prep. Time: 15 minutes ♣ Cooking Time: 6–8 hours ♣ Ideal slow-cooker size: 3-qt.

2 lbs. fully cooked kielbasa sausage, cut into 1-inch pieces

¾ cup brown sugar

1 cup chunky applesauce

2 cloves garlic, minced

1. Combine all ingredients in slow cooker.

2. Cover and cook on Low 6–8 hours, until thoroughly heated.

Sausages in Wine

Mary E. Wheatley, Mashpee, MA

Makes 6 servings or 24 appetizers
Prep. Time: 15 minutes ⚘ Cooking Time: 45 minutes–1 hour ⚘ Ideal slow-cooker size: 3-qt.

1 cup dry red wine

2 Tbsp. currant jelly

6–8 mild Italian sausages or
Polish sausages

1. Place wine and jelly in slow cooker. Heat until jelly is dissolved and sauce begins to simmer. Add sausages.

2. Cover and cook on High 45 minutes to 1 hour, or until sausages are cooked through and lightly glazed.

3. Transfer sausages to a cutting board and slice. Serve with juices spooned over.

Orange Glazed Meatballs

Hope Comerford, Clinton Township, MI

Makes 8–10 servings
Prep. Time: 10 minutes   ❦   Cooking Time: 5 hours   ❦   Ideal slow-cooker size: 5-qt.

28-oz. bag frozen meatballs
12-oz. jar orange marmalade
1 jalapeño pepper, seeded and diced
¼ cup orange juice
¼ cup beef stock
1 Tbsp. Worcestershire sauce
¼ tsp. pepper
3–4 green onions, chopped, for garnish

1. Spray crock with nonstick spray.

2. Place meatballs in crock.

3. In a bowl, combine the orange marmalade, jalapeño, orange juice, beef stock, Worcestershire sauce, and pepper.

4. Pour the sauce over the meatballs. Cover and cook on Low for 5 hours.

5. To serve, sprinkle with chopped green onions.

Tangy Meatballs

Penny Blosser, Beavercreek, OH

Makes 50–60 meatballs

Prep. Time: 15 minutes ⚜ *Cooking Time: 2–4 hours* ⚜ *Ideal slow-cooker size: 4-qt.*

2 lbs. precooked meatballs
16-oz. bottle barbecue sauce
8 ozs. grape jelly

1. Place meatballs in slow cooker.

2. Combine barbecue sauce and jelly in a medium-sized mixing bowl.

3. Pour sauce over meatballs and stir well.

4. Cover and cook on High 2 hours, or on Low 4 hours.

5. Turn to Low and serve.

Venetian Stuffed Mushrooms

MarJanita Geigley, Lancaster, PA

Makes 8 servings

Prep. Time: 30 minutes 🔹 *Cooking Time: 1½–2 hours* 🔹 *Ideal slow-cooker size: Oval 6- to 7-qt.*

24 white clean mushrooms

2 Tbsp. olive oil

1 clove garlic

¼ tsp. butter

¼ cup shredded mozzarella cheese

2 Tbsp. Italian bread crumbs

2 tsp. Italian seasoning

¾ tsp. sea salt

¼ tsp. pepper

1. Remove stems from mushroom caps, including the piece of stem inside the cap.

2. Chop up stems.

3. Brush caps with oil and place them in slow cooker, cap side down.

4. Cook stems in garlic and butter until softened in a saucepan.

5. Stir in shredded cheese, bread crumbs, Italian seasoning, sea salt, and pepper.

6. Spoon the mushroom stem mixture into the caps.

7. Cover and cook on Low for 1½–2 hours.

Basil Mint Tea

Nancy T. Dickman, Marblemount, WA

Makes 10 servings
Prep. Time: 10 minutes ❧ Cooking Time: 2 hours ❧ Ideal slow-cooker size: 3-qt.

20 fresh basil leaves, or 3 Tbsp. dried

20 fresh spearmint or peppermint leaves, or 3 Tbsp. dried

10 cups water

¼ cup sugar

1. Place herbs in slow cooker. If using fresh herbs, mash gently with a spoon. If using dried herbs, put in tea-ball infusers or cheesecloth bag.

2. Add water and sugar.

3. Cover and cook on Low for 2 hours, until fragrant and steaming. Serve hot, or chill completely and serve cold.

TIP
Try mixing some lemonade and lemon slices into the chilled tea.

Hot Spiced Cherry Cider

Jessalyn Wantland, Paris, TX

Makes 10 servings

Prep. Time: 5 minutes ❧ *Cooking Time: 4 hours* ❧ *Ideal slow-cooker size: 4- to 6-qt.*

2 cinnamon sticks

3½ quarts apple cider

3-oz. pkg. cherry-flavored gelatin

1. In slow cooker, add cinnamon sticks to apple cider and stir.

2. Cover and heat on High 3 hours.

3. Stir in gelatin. Cover and leave on High for 1 hour, until gelatin dissolves, stirring once or twice.

4. Turn on Low to keep warm. Remove cinnamon sticks before serving.

TIP

For a more intense cherry flavor, add an additional package of gelatin.

Soups, Stews & Chilies

Broccoli Cheese Soup

Hope Comerford, Clinton Township, MI

Makes 6 servings
Prep. Time: 15 minutes ❧ *Cooking Time: 6–7 hours* ❧ *Ideal slow-cooker size: 3-qt.*

1 head broccoli, chopped into tiny pieces

1 onion, chopped finely

2 12-oz. cans evaporated milk

10 ¾-oz. can condensed cheddar cheese soup

3 cups water

4 chicken bouillon cubes

1½ tsp. garlic powder

1 tsp. onion powder

½ tsp. seasoned salt

1 tsp. pepper

16-oz. block Velveeta cheese, chopped into pieces

1. Place all ingredients into crock, except for the Velveeta cheese, and stir.

2. Cover and cook on Low for 6–7 hours.

3. About 5–10 minutes before eating, turn slow cooker to High and stir in Velveeta cheese until melted.

Fresh Tomato Soup

Rebecca Leichty, Harrisonburg, VA

Makes 6 servings

Prep. Time: 20–25 minutes ⚬ Cooking Time: 3–4 hours ⚬ Ideal slow-cooker size: 3½- to 4-qt.

5 cups diced ripe tomatoes (your choice about whether or not to peel them)

1 Tbsp. tomato paste

4 cups salt-free chicken broth

1 carrot, grated

1 onion, minced

1 Tbsp. minced garlic

1 tsp. dried basil

Pepper, to taste

2 Tbsp. lemon juice

1 dried bay leaf

1. Combine all ingredients in a slow cooker.

2. Cook on Low for 3–4 hours. Stir once while cooking.

3. Remove bay leaf before serving.

Chicken and Vegetable Soup with Rice

Hope Comerford, Clinton Township, MI

Makes 4–6 servings

Prep. Time: 20 minutes & Cooking Time: 6½–7½ hours & Ideal slow-cooker size: 3-qt.

1½–2 lbs. boneless, skinless chicken breasts

1½ cups chopped carrots

1½ cups chopped red onion

2 Tbsp. garlic powder

1 Tbsp. onion powder

2 tsp. salt (you can omit the salt if you're using regular stock rather than no-salt)

¼ tsp. celery seed

¼ tsp. paprika

⅛ tsp. pepper

1 dried bay leaf

8 cups no-salt chicken stock

1 cup fresh green beans

3 cups cooked rice

1. Place chicken into the bottom of crock, then add rest of the remaining ingredients, except green beans and rice.

2. Cover and cook on Low for 6–7 hours.

3. Remove chicken and chop into bite-sized cubes. Place chicken back into crock and add in green beans. Cover and cook another 30 minutes.

4. To serve, place approximately ½ cup of the cooked rice into each bowl and ladle soup over top of the rice.

Italiano Chicken, Rice, and Tomato Soup

Jane Geigley, Lancaster, PA

Makes 6 servings

Prep. Time: 30 minutes ❦ *Cooking Time: 4–6 hours* ❦ *Ideal slow-cooker size: 4-qt.*

½ cup chopped onion

2 Tbsp. butter, softened

½ tsp. paprika

½ tsp. basil

⅛ tsp. garlic powder

8-oz. brick cream cheese, softened

1¼ cups milk

2 10¾-oz. cans tomato soup

2 16-oz. cans whole tomatoes, undrained

1 cup instant rice

2 cups cooked chopped chicken

1 cup shredded mozzarella cheese

1. In a stand mixer, mix the first 9 ingredients. Beat until smooth. Pour into the slow cooker.

2. Stir in rice and chicken.

3. Cover and cook on Low for 4–6 hours. Add the shredded cheese at the very end, just before serving.

Chicken Tortilla Soup

Amy Troyer, Garden Grove, IA

Makes 8 cups

Prep. Time: 30 minutes 🍂 Cooking Time: 3 hours 🍂 Ideal slow-cooker size: 4-qt.

2 Tbsp. olive oil

¾ cup chopped onion

¼ cup chopped carrots

¼ cup chopped celery

¼ cup chopped sweet pepper (green or red)

I clove garlic, minced

½ tsp. chili powder

½ tsp. paprika

½ tsp. dried oregano

I tsp. cumin

I tsp. coriander, *optional*

Dash of red pepper

1½ cups shredded chicken

I qt. chicken broth

I cup water

½ cup fresh chunked tomatoes

1½ tsp. salt

½ tsp. pepper

½ cup cream

I cup shredded cheddar cheese

Crushed tortilla chips, for serving

1. Heat oil in a saucepan and sauté onion, carrots, celery, and peppers.

2. Add the garlic and spices and fry together for 1–2 minutes.

3. In slow cooker, place the sautéed vegetables, chicken, chicken broth, water, tomatoes, salt, and pepper.

4. Cover and cook for 3 hours on Low.

5. Add cream and cheese. Stir until cheese is melted.

6. Serve with crushed tortilla chips.

Serving suggestion:

If you would like to make this soup more of a hearty main-dish soup, add ¾ cup frozen corn and 1 can white kidney beans, drained, toward the end of cooking time (just long enough to cook the corn and warm the beans).

Turkey Rosemary Veggie Soup

Willard E. Roth, Elkhart, IN

Makes 8 servings
Prep. Time: 30 minutes ⚓ *Cooking Time: 8 hours* ⚓ *Ideal slow-cooker size: 6-qt.*

1 lb. 99% fat-free ground turkey
3 parsley stalks with leaves, sliced
3 scallions, chopped
3 medium carrots, unpeeled, sliced
3 medium potatoes, unpeeled, sliced
3 celery ribs with leaves, sliced
3 small onions, sliced
16-oz. can whole-kernel corn, undrained
16-oz. can green beans, undrained
16-oz. can low-sodium diced Italian-style tomatoes
3 cans water
3 packets dry Herb-Ox vegetable broth
1 Tbsp. dried rosemary

1. Brown turkey with parsley and scallions in nonstick skillet. Drain. Pour into slow cooker sprayed with nonstick spray.

2. Add vegetables, water, dry vegetable broth, and rosemary.

3. Cover. Cook on Low 8 hours, or until vegetables are done to your liking.

Cabbage and Beef Soup

Colleen Heatwole, Burton, MI

Makes 6–8 servings
Prep. Time: 20 minutes ⚜ *Cooking Time: 6–8 hours* ⚜ *Ideal slow-cooker size: 6-qt.*

1 lb. lean ground beef

28- or 32-oz. can tomatoes or 1 qt. home-canned tomatoes

¼ tsp. onion powder

1 tsp. garlic powder

¼ tsp pepper

16-oz. can kidney beans, undrained

2 ribs celery, chopped

½ head of cabbage, chopped

4 cups water

4 beef bouillon cubes

Chopped fresh parsley, for garnish

1. Brown beef in large skillet. Add tomatoes and chop coarsely. Transfer to slow cooker.

2. Add remaining ingredients except parsley.

3. Cover and cook 6–8 hours on Low.

4. Serve in bowls garnished with fresh parsley.

TIP

Lean ground turkey may be used. Black beans or small red beans may be substituted for the kidney beans. This soup freezes well.

Taco Bean Soup

Colleen Heatwole, Burton, MI

Makes 8–10 servings
Prep. Time: 20 minutes ⚜ Cooking Time: 4–6 hours ⚜ Ideal slow-cooker size: 6-qt.

1 lb. ground beef

1 large onion, chopped

14-oz. can pinto beans, undrained

15-oz. can black beans, undrained

15-oz. can kidney beans, undrained

2 14½-oz. cans peeled and diced tomatoes or 1 qt. fresh tomatoes

15-oz. can tomato sauce

4-oz. can diced green chilies

1 pkg. dry taco seasoning

15-oz. can whole-kernel corn, undrained

1. Brown beef and onion in skillet. Drain if needed. (Not needed if beef is extremely low fat.)

2. Place beef mixture in slow cooker along with other ingredients.

3. Cook on Low 4–6 hours.

Serving suggestion:

Serve with sour cream, grated cheese, and tortilla chips.

TIP

Any beans can be used in this recipe. You can keep frozen beans that you have cooked on hand and just use a combination.

Zucchini Stew

Colleen Heatwole, Burton, MI

Makes 6 servings
Prep. Time: 30 minutes ⚘ *Cooking Time: 4–6 hours* ⚘ *Ideal slow-cooker size: 6-qt.*

1 lb. Italian sausage, sliced
2 ribs of celery, diced
2 medium green bell peppers, diced
1 medium onion, chopped
2 28-oz. cans diced tomatoes
2 lbs. zucchini, cut into ½-inch slices
2 cloves garlic, minced
1 tsp. sugar
1 tsp. dried oregano
1 tsp. Italian seasoning
1 tsp. salt, *optional* (taste first)
6 Tbsp. grated Parmesan cheese

1. Brown sausage in hot skillet until brown and crumbly, about 5–7 minutes. Drain and discard grease.

2. Mix celery, bell peppers, and onion into cooked sausage and cook and stir until they are softened, 10–12 minutes.

3. Combine remaining ingredients, except Parmesan cheese, and add to slow cooker.

4. Cook on Low 4–6 hours. Garnish each serving with 1 Tbsp. Parmesan cheese.

Serving suggestion:
Croutons can be added to individual bowls for some crunch.

Chili Chicken Stew with Rice

Jenny R. Unternahrer, Wayland, IA

Makes 4–5 servings

Prep. Time: 30 minutes   ⚬   Cooking Time: 2½–5 hours   ⚬   Ideal slow-cooker size: 2½-qt.

1½ lbs. chicken tenders*

½ small onion, diced

15-oz. can black beans, drained (not rinsed)

14½-oz. can petite diced tomatoes, undrained

1 cup whole corn, drained if needed (thawed if frozen)

2 tsp. chili powder

½ tsp. cumin

2–4 dashes cayenne pepper

1½ tsp. salt

2 cups cooked brown rice

Sour cream, to taste

Shredded Mexican blend cheese, to taste

---

*You can try whole boneless, skinless chicken breast, but allow more time to cook.

1. Add all the ingredients, except brown rice, sour cream, and shredded cheese, to crock.

2. Mix. Cover and cook on High for 2½ hours or Low for 5 hours.

3. Shred chicken; stir to incorporate.

4. Serve over brown rice and add desired amount of sour cream and shredded Mexican blend cheese.

Cider Beef Stew

Jean Turner, Williams Lake, BC

Makes 8 servings
Prep. Time: 30 minutes ❧ Cooking Time: 8–10 hours ❧ Ideal slow-cooker size: 3-qt.

2 lbs. stewing beef, cut into 1-inch cubes

6 Tbsp. flour, *divided*

2 tsp. salt

¼ tsp. pepper

¼ tsp. dried thyme

3 Tbsp. cooking oil

4 potatoes, peeled and quartered

4 carrots, quartered

2 onions, sliced

1 rib celery, sliced

1 apple, chopped

2 cups apple cider or apple juice

1–2 Tbsp. vinegar

½ cup cold water

1. Stir together beef, 3 Tbsp. flour, salt, pepper, and thyme. Brown coated beef in oil in skillet. Do in two batches if necessary to avoid crowding the meat.

2. Place vegetables and apple in slow cooker. Place browned meat cubes on top.

3. Pour apple cider and vinegar over everything.

4. Cover and cook on Low for 8–10 hours.

5. Turn slow cooker to High. Blend cold water with remaining 3 Tbsp. flour. Stir into hot stew.

6. Cover and cook on High for 15 minutes, or until thickened.

Serving suggestion:
A side salad is all that is needed for a complete meal.

Nutritious Tasty Beef Stew

Annie Boshart, Lititz, PA

Makes 8 servings
Prep. Time: 30 minutes ☙ *Cooking Time: 4 hours* ☙ *Ideal slow-cooker size: 6-qt.*

3-lb. rump roast, or your choice of beef

4 carrots, cut into serving-sized pieces

8 potatoes, peeled and cut into bite-sized pieces

¼ cup chopped red onion

¼ cup chopped white onion

2 cups fresh salsa

2 Tbsp. instant tapioca

1 Tbsp. Worcestershire sauce

1. Place rump roast or choice of beef in slow cooker.

2. Add the vegetables to slow cooker.

3. Mix together the salsa, tapioca, and Worcestershire sauce. Pour on top of vegetables.

4. Cover and cook on High for 4 hours.

TIP
Fresh salsa is made with fresh herbs, tomatoes, and other desired ingredients—vinegar, lemon juice, and cilantro to taste. This can also be frozen or canned.

Cider and Pork Stew

Veronica Sabo, Shelton, CT

Makes 5 servings
Prep. Time: 15 minutes ❧ Cooking Time: 7–9 hours ❧ Ideal slow-cooker size: 3½-qt.

2 medium (about 1¼ lbs.) sweet potatoes, peeled if you wish, and cut into ¾-inch pieces

3 small carrots, peeled and cut into ½-inch-thick slices

1 cup chopped onion

1–2-lb. boneless pork shoulder, cut into 1-inch cubes

1 large Granny Smith apple, peeled, cored, and coarsely chopped

¼ cup flour

¾ tsp. salt

½ tsp. dried sage

½ tsp. thyme

½ tsp. pepper

1 cup apple cider

1. Layer sweet potatoes, carrots, onions, pork, and apple in slow cooker.

2. Combine flour, salt, sage, thyme, and pepper in medium bowl.

3. Add cider to flour mixture. Stir until smooth.

4. Pour cider mixture over meat and vegetables in slow cooker.

5. Cover. Cook on Low 7–9 hours, or until meat and vegetables are tender.

Summer Chili

Hope Comerford, Clinton Township, MI

Makes 6 servings
Prep. Time: 15 minutes & Cooking Time: 3½–4 hours & Ideal slow-cooker size: 3-qt.

28-oz. can Red Gold sliced tomatoes and zucchini

15-oz. can tomato sauce

14-oz. can petite diced tomatoes with green chilies

15½-oz. can chili beans

15¼-oz. can black beans, drained and rinsed

1 medium onion, roughly chopped

3 small yellow squash, halved, quartered, and chopped

3 Tbsp. garlic powder

2 Tbsp. onion powder

1 tsp. salt

⅛ tsp. pepper

2 cups water

1. Place all ingredients into crock and stir.

2. Cover and cook on Low for 3½–4 hours.

White Bean and Chicken Chili

Hope Comerford, Clinton Township, MI

Makes 6–8 servings

Prep. Time: 15 minutes ❧ *Cooking Time: 8–10 hours* ❧ *Ideal slow-cooker size: 5-qt.*

2 lbs. boneless, skinless chicken, cut into bite-sized chunks

½ cup dry navy beans, soaked overnight, drained, and rinsed

½ cup dry great northern beans, soaked overnight, drained, and rinsed

½ cup chopped carrots

1½ cups chopped onion

14½-oz. can petite diced tomatoes

10-oz. can diced tomatoes with lime juice and cilantro

5 cloves garlic, minced

6-oz. can tomato paste

1 Tbsp. cumin

1 Tbsp. chili powder

1 tsp. salt

¼ tsp. pepper

8 tsp. Better than Bouillon chicken base

8 cups water

1. Place all ingredients into the crock and stir to mix well.

2. Cover and cook on Low for 8–10 hours.

Chicken Chili

Sharon Miller, Holmesville, OH

Makes 6 servings

Prep. Time: 15 minutes & Cooking Time: 5–6 hours & Ideal slow-cooker size: 4-qt.

2 lbs. boneless, skinless chicken breasts, cubed

2 Tbsp. butter

2 14-oz. cans diced tomatoes, undrained

15-oz. can red kidney beans, rinsed and drained

1 cup diced onion

1 cup diced red bell pepper

1–2 Tbsp. chili powder, according to your taste preference

1 tsp. cumin

1 tsp. dried oregano

Salt and pepper, to taste

1. In skillet on high heat, brown chicken cubes in butter until they have some browned edges. Place in greased slow cooker.

2. Pour one of the cans of tomatoes with its juice into skillet to get all the browned bits and butter. Scrape and pour into slow cooker.

3. Add rest of ingredients, including other can of tomatoes, to cooker.

4. Cook on Low for 5–6 hours.

Serving suggestion:

You can serve this chili with shredded cheddar cheese and sour cream.

Chicken Barley Chili

Colleen Heatwole, Burton, MI

Makes 10 servings

Prep. Time: 20 minutes & Cooking Time: 6–8 hours & Ideal slow-cooker size: 6-qt.

2 14½-oz. cans diced tomatoes

16-oz. jar salsa

1 cup quick-cooking barley

3 cups water

14½-oz. can chicken broth

15½-oz. can black beans, rinsed and drained

3 cups cooked chicken or turkey, cubed

15¼-oz. can whole-kernel corn, undrained

1–3 tsp. chili powder, depending on how hot you like your chili

1 tsp. cumin

1. Combine all ingredients in slow cooker.

2. Cover. Cook on Low 6–8 hours, or until barley is tender.

Serving suggestion:

Serve in individual soup bowls topped with sour cream and shredded cheese.

Any Bean, Any Burger Chili

Colleen Heatwole, Burton, MI

Makes 6–8 servings

Prep. Time: 30 minutes   ⚓   Cooking Time: 5–6 hours   ⚓   Ideal slow-cooker size: 5-qt.

2 medium onions, coarsely chopped

1–1½ lbs. ground beef

¾ cup finely diced green peppers

2 cloves garlic, minced fine

2 Tbsp. olive oil

2 14½-oz. cans diced tomatoes or 1 qt. canned tomatoes

30–32 ozs. beans (pinto, kidney, black, or any mixture of the three)

8-oz. can tomato sauce

1 tsp. cumin

½ tsp. pepper

1 tsp. seasoned salt

1 Tbsp. chili powder

1 tsp. dried basil

½ tsp. Spice Islands Beau Monde seasoning

1. Brown onions, beef, green peppers, and garlic in saucepan with the olive oil. Drain, unless beef is low in fat.

2. Combine all ingredients in slow cooker.

3. Cover and cook on Low 5–6 hours.

TIP

About twenty years ago, Beau Monde seasoning was readily available but is not now, although it can be ordered. This recipe is fine without it, although it is even better with it. Any combination of beans can be used. You can also make this chili with ground venison, ground turkey, ground elk, or even ground bear! If you are fortunate to know someone who hunts, the burger will work in this recipe.

Chili in a Slow Cooker

Jo Zimmerman, Lebanon, PA

Makes 6 servings
Prep. Time: 15–30 minutes   ♣   Cooking Time: 6 hours   ♣   Ideal slow-cooker size: 5-qt.

1½ lbs. ground beef
1 medium onion, chopped
1 green pepper, chopped
½ tsp. garlic powder
14½-oz. can of diced tomatoes
2 5½-oz. cans V8 juice
1 Tbsp. chili powder
Pinch of red pepper flakes

1. Place all ingredients in crock and stir.

2. Cover and cook on Low for 6 hours.

Serving suggestion:

This pairs well with cornbread.

Kale Chowder

Colleen Heatwole, Burton, MI

Makes 8 servings
Prep. Time: 30 minutes ⚜ *Cooking Time: 6 hours* ⚜ *Ideal slow-cooker size: 6-qt.*

8 cups chicken broth

1 bunch of kale, cleaned, stems removed, and chopped

2 lbs. potatoes, peeled and diced

4 cloves garlic, minced

1 onion, diced

1 lb. cooked ham

½ tsp. pepper, or to taste

1. Combine all ingredients in slow cooker.

2. Cover and cook on Low 6 hours, or until vegetables are tender.

TIP
If you are using new potatoes, peeling is optional.

Corn Chowder

Colleen Heatwole, Burton, MI

Makes 8 servings
Prep. Time: 20 minutes ⚜ *Cooking Time: 5–6 hours* ⚜ *Ideal slow-cooker size: 3½-qt.*

½ cup diced cooked bacon, drippings reserved

4 cups peeled, chopped potatoes (about 4 medium potatoes)

1 medium onion, chopped

2 cups water

2 14½-oz. cans cream-style corn

1 tsp. salt

½ tsp. pepper

2 cups half-and-half

1. Add bacon and the bacon drippings to slow cooker.

2. Add potatoes, onion, water, corn, salt, and pepper.

3. Cover and cook on Low for 5–6 hours, until potatoes and onions are soft.

4. Warm half-and-half in saucepan or microwave until steaming hot. Do not boil. Add half-and-half to chowder just before serving.

Serving suggestion:

A garnish of fresh parsley makes this dish sparkle!

Sausage and Kale Chowder

Beverly Hummel, Fleetwood, PA

Makes 6 servings
Prep. Time: 20 minutes   Cooking Time: 5 hours   Ideal slow-cooker size: 4- to 5-qt.

1 lb. bulk sausage
1 cup chopped onion
6 small red potatoes, chopped
1 cup thinly sliced kale, ribs removed
6 cups chicken broth
1 cup milk, at room temperature
Salt and pepper, to taste

1. Brown sausage. Drain off grease. Transfer sausage to slow cooker.

2. Add onion, potatoes, kale, and broth.

3. Cook on High for 4 hours, until potatoes and kale are soft.

4. Add milk and cook on Low for 1 hour. Season to taste with salt and pepper.

TIP

If you prefer a thicker soup, add 2 Tbsp. cornstarch to milk in Step 4 before adding to cooker. Stir several times in the last hour as chowder thickens.

Serving suggestion:
Italian bread and salad make a great accompaniment to this chowder.

Oceanside Bisque

Jane Geigley, Lancaster, PA

Makes 8 servings

Prep. Time: 30 minutes ⚜ *Cooking Time: 2–3 hours* ⚜ *Ideal slow-cooker size: 6-qt.*

1 Tbsp. unsalted butter

1 Tbsp. canola oil

3 large shallots, minced (or 1 Vidalia onion, minced)

5 cups chicken stock

2 cups heavy cream

1 Tbsp. kosher salt

½ tsp. freshly ground white pepper

1 lb. fresh or thawed lump crabmeat (picked over for shell fragments), or canned crabmeat

½ cup dry sherry

Fresh tarragon or flat-leaf parsley for garnish

1. In small saucepan, melt butter and oil over medium heat.

2. Add shallots and sauté until translucent (about 2–3 minutes).

3. Pour into slow cooker.

4. Add stock and cream.

5. Season with salt and pepper.

6. Cook on High for ½ hour.

7. Add crabmeat and sherry.

8. Stir.

9. Cook for another 2–3 hours.

10. Ladle into bowls and garnish with tarragon or parsley.

Serving suggestion:

Serve with oyster crackers and cubed cheese. This is also delicious with fresh chopped parsley on top and a sprinkle of turmeric or paprika.

Main Dishes

Easy Slow Cooker Italian Chicken

Gwendolyn Muholland, Corryton, TN

Makes 4–6 servings
Prep. Time: 5–20 minutes ♣ Cooking Time: 4–8 hours ♣ Ideal slow-cooker size: 4-qt.

2–3 boneless, skinless
chicken breasts

23½-oz. jar Prego
Traditional Italian sauce

14½-oz. jar Prego
Homestyle Alfredo sauce

1 cup shredded mozzarella cheese

16-oz. box pasta

1. Place the uncooked chicken breasts in the bottom of the slow cooker.

2. Top with Italian sauce, Alfredo sauce, and shredded mozzarella.

3. Cover and cook on Low for 6–8 hours or High for 4 hours.

4. When you're ready to eat, cook pasta according to the directions on the package.

5. Serve chicken on top of pasta with sauce.

TIP

Cook pasta right before serving, or cook it the night before and warm it up before serving.

Serving suggestion:
This dish goes well with garlic bread and salad.

Cranberry Chicken Barbecue

Gladys M. High, Ephrata, PA

Makes 6–8 servings
Prep. Time: 10 minutes ♣ Cooking Time: 4–8 hours ♣ Ideal slow-cooker size: 4- to 5-qt.

4 lbs. chicken pieces, *divided*

½ tsp. salt

¼ tsp. pepper

16-oz. can whole-berry cranberry sauce

1 cup barbecue sauce

½ cup diced celery, *optional*

½ cup diced onion, *optional*

1. Place ⅓ of chicken pieces in slow cooker.

2. Combine all sauce ingredients in a mixing bowl. Spoon ⅓ of the sauce over the chicken in the cooker. Include celery and onions if you like.

3. Repeat Steps 1 and 2 twice.

4. Cover and cook on High 4 hours, or on Low 6–8 hours, or until chicken is tender but not dry.

Orange Garlic Chicken

Susan Kasting, Jenks, OK

Makes 6 servings
Prep. Time: 15 minutes ♣ Cooking Time: 2½–6 hours ♣ Ideal slow-cooker size: 4-qt.

1 ½ tsp. dried thyme

6 cloves garlic, minced

6 skinless bone-in chicken breast halves

1 cup orange juice concentrate

2 Tbsp. balsamic vinegar

1. Rub thyme and garlic over chicken. (Reserve any leftover thyme and garlic.) Place chicken in slow cooker.

2. Mix orange juice concentrate and vinegar together in a small bowl. Stir in reserved thyme and garlic. Spoon over chicken.

3. Cover and cook on Low 5–6 hours, or on High 2½–3 hours, or until chicken is tender but not dry.

Orange Glazed Chicken Breasts

Corinna Herr, Stevens, PA ⚜ *Karen Ceneviva, New Haven, CT*

Makes 6 servings
Prep. Time: 15 minutes ⚜ Cooking Time: 4–9 hours ⚜ Ideal slow-cooker size: 4-qt.

12 ozs. orange juice concentrate, undiluted and thawed

½ tsp. dried marjoram leaves

6 boneless, skinless chicken breast halves

Salt and pepper, to taste

¼ cup water

2 Tbsp. cornstarch

1. Combine thawed orange juice and marjoram in shallow dish. Dip each breast in orange juice mixture.

2. Sprinkle each breast with salt and pepper; place in slow cooker.

3. Cover and cook on Low 6½–8½ hours, or on High 3½–4½ hours, or until chicken is tender but not dry.

4. Half an hour before serving, remove chicken breasts from slow cooker and keep warm on a platter.

5. Mix water and cornstarch together in a small bowl until smooth. Turn slow cooker to High. Stir cornstarch mixture into liquid in slow cooker.

6. Place cover slightly ajar on slow cooker. Cook until sauce is thickened and bubbly, about 15–30 minutes. Serve sauce over chicken.

Chicken and Egg Noodle Dinner

Janie Steele, Moore, OK

Makes 5–7 servings
Prep. Time: 15 minutes   ⚜   Cooking Time: 5–6 hours   ⚜   Ideal slow-cooker size: 5-qt.

1 14-oz. can low-sodium cream of chicken soup

2 15½-oz. cans low-sodium chicken broth

1 tsp. garlic powder

1 tsp. onion powder

¼ tsp. celery seed

¼ tsp. pepper

4 Tbsp. butter or margarine

1 lb. boneless, skinless chicken breasts

24-oz. bag frozen egg noodles

1. Place all ingredients in crock except the noodles.

2. Cover and cook for 5–6 hours on Low.

3. Remove chicken and shred. Return to slow cooker, then add frozen noodles and cook for an additional 40–60 minutes, or until noodles are tender.

Creamy Italian Chicken

Jo Zimmerman, Lebanon, PA

Makes 6 servings
Prep. Time: 10 minutes 🍃 Cooking Time: 4 hours 🍃 Ideal slow-cooker size: 3-qt.

2 lbs. chicken tenders
1 envelope Italian salad dressing mix
¼ cup water
8-oz. pkg. cream cheese
1 can cream of chicken soup
1 can of mushrooms drained, *optional*

1. Place chicken in slow cooker.

2. Combine dressing mix and water. Pour over chicken.

3. Cover and cook on Low 3 hours.

4. Beat cream cheese and soup together and stir in mushrooms if you like. Pour over chicken and cook 1 hour longer.

Serving suggestion:

Serve over rice.

Chicken and Dressing

Sharon Miller, Holmesville, OH

Makes 10–12 servings
Prep. Time: 30 minutes ⚜ Cooking Time: 4¾ hours–8¾ hours ⚜ Ideal slow-cooker size: 6-qt.

12–13 cups slightly dry bread cubes
1–2 cups chopped onion
2 cups diced celery
8 Tbsp. butter, melted
1 tsp. poultry seasoning
½ tsp. dried thyme
1½ tsp. salt
½ tsp. pepper
3 cups shredded or diced cooked chicken
3 well-beaten eggs
3½–4½ cups chicken broth

1. Place bread cubes in a large bowl.

2. Sauté onion and celery in melted butter. Stir in poultry seasoning, thyme, salt, and pepper.

3. Toss in the cooked chicken.

4. Pour entire chicken mixture over bread cubes and toss well together.

5. Add the eggs.

6. Stir in chicken broth to moisten. Pack lightly into slow cooker.

7. Cover and cook on High for 45 minutes. Reduce heat to Low and cook 4–8 hours.

Serving suggestion:

A green vegetable and cranberry sauce would make a nice accompaniment to this dish.

TIP
This dish is ideal for a Thanksgiving meal as it does not tie up the oven.

Slow Cooker Chicken and Dumplings

Kris Zimmerman, Lititz, PA

Makes 8–10 servings

Prep. Time: 15 minutes ☙ Cooking Time: 5–7 hours ☙ Ideal slow-cooker size: 5-qt.

4–6 boneless, skinless chicken breasts

2 Tbsp. butter, melted

2 10½-oz. cans cream of chicken soup

1 onion, diced

14-oz. can chicken broth

1 Tbsp. dried parsley

16.3-oz. pkg. Pillsbury Grands! biscuits

1. Place chicken breasts, butter, soup, onion, chicken broth, and parsley in crock.

2. Cover and cook on High for 4–6 hours.

3. After 4–6 hours, break chicken up using 2 forks or tongs.

4. Cut biscuits into small pieces. Kitchen shears work great for this.

5. Stir biscuits into chicken and cook on High for an additional 40–50 minutes.

TIP
Steamed carrots go great with this.

Honey Baked Chicken

Mary Kennell, Roanoke, IL

Makes 4 servings
Prep. Time: 15 minutes ⚭ Cooking Time: 3–6 hours ⚭ Ideal slow-cooker size: 5-qt.

4 skinless bone-in chicken breast halves

2 Tbsp. butter, melted

2 Tbsp. honey

2 tsp. prepared mustard

2 tsp. curry powder

Salt and pepper, *optional*

1. Spray slow cooker with nonstick spray and add chicken.

2. Mix butter, honey, mustard, and curry powder together in a small bowl. Pour sauce over chicken.

3. Cover and cook on High 3 hours, or on Low 5–6 hours.

Bacon-Feta Stuffed Chicken

Tina Goss, Duenweg, MO

Makes 4 servings
Prep. Time: 10 minutes ☙ Cooking Time: 1½–3 hours ☙ Ideal slow-cooker size: 3-qt.

¼ cup crumbled cooked bacon

¼ cup crumbled feta cheese

4 boneless, skinless chicken breast halves

2 14½-oz. cans diced tomatoes, undrained

1 Tbsp. dried basil

1. In a small bowl, mix bacon and cheese together lightly.

2. Cut a pocket in the thicker side of each chicken breast. Fill each with ¼ of the bacon and cheese mixture. Pinch shut and secure with toothpicks.

3. Place chicken in slow cooker. Top with tomatoes and sprinkle with basil.

4. Cover and cook on High 1½–3 hours, or until chicken is tender but not dry or mushy.

Apricot Stuffing and Chicken

Elizabeth Colucci, Lancaster, PA

Makes 5 servings
Prep. Time: 10 minutes ⚬ *Cooking Time: 2–3½ hours* ⚬ *Ideal slow-cooker size: 5-qt.*

1 stick (8 Tbsp.) butter, *divided*

1 box cornbread stuffing mix

4 boneless, skinless chicken breast halves

6–8-oz. jar apricot preserves

1. In a mixing bowl, make stuffing using ½ stick (4 Tbsp.) butter and amount of water called for in instructions on box. Set aside.

2. Cut up chicken into 1-inch pieces. Place on bottom of slow cooker. Spoon stuffing over top.

3. In microwave or on stovetop, melt remaining ½ stick (4 Tbsp.) butter with preserves. Pour over stuffing.

4. Cover and cook on High for 2 hours, or on Low for 3½ hours, or until chicken is tender but not dry.

Chicken Parmigiana

Lois Ostrander, Lebanon, PA

Makes 6 servings
Prep. Time: 20 minutes   ⚬   Cooking Time: 6–8 hours   ⚬   Ideal slow-cooker size: 3½-qt.

I egg

I cup dry bread crumbs

6 bone-in chicken breast halves, *divided*

10½-oz. jar pizza sauce, *divided*

6 slices mozzarella cheese, or ½ cup grated Parmesan cheese

1. Beat egg in a shallow, oblong bowl. Place bread crumbs in another shallow, oblong bowl. Dip chicken halves into egg, and then into the crumbs, using a spoon to coat the meat on all sides with crumbs.

2. Sauté chicken in a large nonstick skillet sprayed with nonstick spray.

3. Arrange 1 layer of browned chicken in slow cooker. Pour half the pizza sauce over top. Add a second layer of chicken. Pour remaining pizza sauce over top.

4. Cover and cook on Low 5¾–7¾ hours, or until chicken is tender but not dry.

5. Add cheese on top. Cover and cook 15 more minutes.

Roast Chicken or Hen

Betty Drescher, Quakertown, PA

Makes 6 servings
Prep. Time: 30 minutes   ⚶   Cooking Time: 9–11 hours   ⚶   Ideal slow-cooker size: 4- to 5-qt.

3–4-lb. roasting chicken or hen
1½ tsp. salt
¼ tsp. pepper
1 tsp. dried parsley flakes, *divided*
1 Tbsp. butter
½–1 cup water

1. Thoroughly wash chicken and pat dry.

2. Sprinkle cavity with salt, pepper, and ½ tsp. parsley flakes. Place in slow cooker, breast side up.

3. Dot with butter or brush with melted butter.

4. Sprinkle with remaining parsley flakes. Add water around the chicken.

5. Cover and cook on High 1 hour. Turn to Low and cook 8–10 hours.

TIPS

1. Sprinkle with basil or tarragon in Step 4, if you wish.

2. To make this dish a more complete meal, put carrots, onions, and celery in the bottom of the slow cooker.

Maple-Glazed Turkey Breast with Rice

Jeanette Oberholtzer, Manheim, PA

Makes 4 servings

Prep. Time: 10–15 minutes ⚬ *Cooking Time: 4–6 hours* ⚬ *Ideal slow-cooker size: 3- to 4-qt.*

6-oz. pkg. long-grain wild rice mix

1 ½ cups water

2-lb. boneless turkey breast, cut into 1 ½–2-inch chunks

¼ cup maple syrup

1 onion, chopped

¼ tsp. cinnamon

½ tsp. salt, *optional*

1. Combine all ingredients in the slow cooker.

2. Cook on Low 4–6 hours, or until turkey and rice are both tender but not dry or mushy.

Traditional Turkey Breast

Hope Comerford, Clinton Township, MI

Makes 10–12 servings
Prep. Time: 10 minutes ❧ Cooking Time: 8 hours ❧ Ideal slow-cooker size: 7-qt.

7-lb. or less turkey breast

olive oil

½ stick butter

Rub:

2 tsp. garlic powder

1 tsp. onion powder

1 tsp. salt

¼ tsp. pepper

1 tsp. poultry seasoning

1. Remove gizzards from turkey breast, rinse it, and pat dry. Place breast into crock.

2. Rub turkey breast all over with olive oil.

3. Cut the butter into 8 pieces. Mix together all rub ingredients. Rub this mixture all over turkey breast and press it in.

4. Place the pieces of butter all over top of the breast.

5. Cover and cook on Low for 8 hours.

Serving suggestion:

Serve with mashed potatoes, cranberry sauce, and stuffing.

Onion Mushroom Pot Roast

Deb Herr, Mountaintop, PA

Makes 6 servings
Prep. Time: 10 minutes 🍃 Cooking Time: 5–12 hours 🍃 Ideal slow-cooker size: 6-qt.

3–4-lb. pot roast or chuck roast

4-oz. can sliced mushrooms, drained

1 tsp. salt

¼ tsp. pepper

½ cup beef broth

1 envelope dry onion soup mix

½ cup flour or cornstarch plus ½ cup water, *optional*

1. Place pot roast in your slow cooker.

2. Add mushrooms, salt, and pepper.

3. In a small bowl, mix beef broth with the onion soup mix. Spoon over the roast.

4. Cover and cook on High 5–6 hours or on Low 10–12 hours, or until meat is tender but not dry.

5. To make gravy, prepare a smooth paste in a jar or small bowl, mixing ½ cup flour or cornstarch with ½ cup water. After the roast is fully cooked, remove the meat and keep it warm on a platter. Turn cooker to High. When juices begin to boil, pour flour/water paste in a thin stream into cooker, stirring continually. Continue cooking and stirring until juices thicken. Serve over sliced roast or in a bowl along with the meat.

Flavorful Pot Roast

Mary Kay Nolt, Newmanstown, PA

Makes 10–12 servings

Prep. Time: 10 minutes ☙ *Cooking Time: 7–8 hours* ☙ *Ideal slow-cooker size: 5-qt.*

2 2½-lb. boneless beef chuck roasts

1 envelope dry ranch salad dressing mix

1 envelope dry Italian salad dressing mix

1 envelope dry brown gravy mix

½ cup water

1 Tbsp. flour plus ½ cup water, *optional*

1. Place the chuck roasts in your slow cooker.

2. In a small bowl, combine the salad dressing and gravy mixes. Stir in water. Pour over the meat.

3. Cover and cook on Low 7–8 hours, or until meat is tender but not dry.

4. Remove meat at end of cooking time and keep warm on a platter. If you wish, thicken the cooking juices for gravy with following steps.

5. Turn cooker to High. Bring juices to a boil.

6. Meanwhile, mix 1 Tbsp. flour with ½ cup water in a jar with a tight-fitting lid. Shake until smooth.

7. When juices come to a boil, pour flour/water mixture into cooker in a thin stream, stirring constantly. Continue cooking and stirring until juices thicken.

8. Serve gravy over meat or in a side dish along with the meat.

Green Chili Roast

Anna Kenagy, Carlsbad, NM

Makes 8–10 servings
Prep. Time: 15 minutes ⚜ Cooking Time: 8 hours ⚜ Ideal slow-cooker size: 4-qt.

3–4-lb. beef roast

1 tsp. seasoned meat tenderizer,
optional

olive oil, *optional*

1 tsp. salt

3–4 green chili peppers, or 4-oz. can
green chilies, undrained

1 Tbsp. Worcestershire sauce

½ tsp. pepper

1. Sprinkle roast with meat tenderizer. Brown roast under broiler or in skillet in oil. Place in slow cooker.

2. Pour in water until roast is half covered.

3. Add remaining ingredients on top.

4. Cover. Cook on Low 8 hours.

Serving suggestion:
Serve with mashed potatoes
and green beans.

Herby French Dip

Sara Wichert, Hillsboro, KS

Makes 6–8 servings
Prep. Time: 5 minutes ⚬ *Cooking Time: 5–6 hours* ⚬ *Ideal slow-cooker size: 4-qt.*

3-lb. chuck roast
2 cups water
½ cup soy sauce
1 tsp. garlic powder
1 dried bay leaf
3–4 whole peppercorns
1 tsp. dried rosemary, *optional*
1 tsp. dried thyme, *optional*
6–8 French rolls

1. Place roast in slow cooker.

2. Combine remaining ingredients in a mixing bowl. Pour over meat.

3. Cover and cook on High 5–6 hours, or until meat is tender but not dry.

4. Remove meat from broth and shred with fork. Stir back into sauce.

5. Remove meat from the cooker by large forkfuls and place on French rolls.

Tostadas

Anita Troyer, Fairview, MI

Makes 6 servings

Prep. Time: 30 minutes   ⚬   Cooking Time: 2 hours   ⚬   Ideal slow-cooker size: 3-qt.

1 lb. ground beef
1 cup diced onion
2 cloves garlic, crushed
2 Tbsp. olive oil
4 cups refried beans
1 tsp. cumin
½ tsp. pepper

1. Brown the beef, onion, and garlic in oil in a skillet.

2. Add all the ingredients into a greased slow cooker.

3. Cover and cook on Low for 2 hours.

Serving suggestion:

Serve with crushed corn chips, tomatoes, lettuce, sour cream, and shredded cheese.

Enchilada Casserole

Hope Comerford, Clinton Township, MI

Makes 8 servings
Prep. Time: 25 minutes ⚭ *Cooking Time: 4–6 hours* ⚭ *Ideal slow-cooker size: 6-qt.*

9 small round flour tortillas, *divided*

1½ lbs. ground beef, browned, *divided*

1 medium onion, chopped, *divided*

2 cups fresh diced tomatoes, *divided*

10-oz. can mild red enchilada sauce, *divided*

2 cups shredded Mexican blend cheese, *divided*

10-oz. can mild green enchilada sauce

1. Spray crock with nonstick spray.

2. Place 3 tortillas in bottom of crock. Cut them if necessary to make them fit.

3. Layer ½ of ground beef on top, followed by ½ the onion, ½ the diced tomatoes, ½ the red enchilada sauce, and ⅓ of the cheese. Repeat this process once more.

4. Finish with final 3 tortillas on top, entire can of green enchilada sauce, and remaining cheese.

5. Cook on Low for 4–6 hours.

Fajita Steak

Becky Harder, Monument, CO

Makes 6 servings

Prep. Time: 10 minutes ⚬ *Cooking Time: 6–8 hours* ⚬ *Ideal slow-cooker size: 4-qt.*

15-oz. can tomatoes with green chilies

¼ cup salsa, your choice of mild, medium, or hot

8-oz. can tomato sauce

2 lbs. round steak, cut in 2 x 4-inch strips

1 envelope dry fajita spice mix

1 cup water, *optional*

1. Combine all ingredients except water in your slow cooker.

2. Cover and cook on Low 6–8 hours, or until meat is tender but not overcooked.

3. Check meat occasionally to make sure it isn't cooking dry. If it begins to look dry, stir in water, up to 1 cup.

Serving suggestion:

Serve meat with fried onions and green peppers. Offer shredded cheese, avocado chunks, and sour cream as toppings. Let individual eaters wrap any or all of the ingredients in flour tortillas.

Mexican Meatloaf

Jennifer Freed, Rockingham, VA

Makes 4–6 servings

Prep. Time: 20 minutes ❧ *Cooking Time: 5–7 hours* ❧ *Ideal slow-cooker size: 3- to 4-qt.*

2 lbs. ground beef

2 cups crushed saltines

1 cup shredded cheddar cheese

⅔ cup salsa

2 eggs, beaten

4 Tbsp. taco seasoning

1. Combine all ingredients in large bowl; mix well.

2. Shape meat mixture into loaf and place in slow cooker.

3. Cover; cook on Low for 5–7 hours, or until internal temperature is 165°F.

Serving suggestion:

For a glaze, mix together ½ cup ketchup, 2 Tbsp. brown sugar, and 1 tsp. dry mustard. Spread over meatloaf. Cover; cook on High 15 minutes.

Carolina Pot Roast

Jonathan Gehman, Harrisonburg, VA

Makes 3–4 servings
Prep. Time: 20 minutes ❧ Cooking Time: 3 hours ❧ Ideal slow-cooker size: 3-qt.

3 medium-large sweet potatoes, peeled and cut into 1-inch chunks

½ cup brown sugar

1-lb. pork roast

Scant ¼ tsp. cumin

Salt, to taste

Water

1. Place sweet potatoes in bottom of slow cooker. Sprinkle brown sugar over potatoes.

2. Heat nonstick skillet over medium-high heat. Add roast and brown on all sides. Sprinkle meat with cumin and salt while browning. Place pork on top of potatoes.

3. Add an inch of water to the cooker, being careful not to wash the seasoning off the meat.

4. Cover and cook on Low 3 hours, or until meat and potatoes are tender but not dry or mushy.

Cranberry Pork Loin

Annabelle Unternahrer, Shipshewana, IN

Makes 6–8 servings
Prep. Time: 10 minutes   ☙   Cooking Time: 4–6 hours   ☙   Ideal slow-cooker size: 5- to 6-qt.

3-lb. boneless pork loin
16-oz. can jellied cranberry sauce
¼ cup sugar
½ cup cranberry juice
1 tsp. dry mustard
¼ tsp. ground cloves, *optional*

1. Place pork loin in slow cooker.

2. Combine remaining ingredients in a bowl. Pour sauce over pork.

3. Cover and cook on Low 4–6 hours, or until meat is tender.

TIP

To thicken the sauce, remove cooked meat to a platter and cover to keep warm. Mix 2 Tbsp. cornstarch with 2 Tbsp. water in a small bowl. Turn cooker to High. Stir cornstarch/water mixture into simmering sauce. Continue stirring until it is thoroughly combined. Then allow sauce to simmer until it thickens, about 10 minutes. Stir occasionally to keep it from getting lumpy. Serve thickened sauce over or alongside pork slices.

Spicy Pork Chops

Cynthia Morris, Grottoes, VA

Makes 4 servings
Prep. Time: 5 minutes & Cooking Time: 6–8 hours & Ideal slow-cooker size: 4-qt.

4 frozen pork chops
1 cup Italian salad dressing
½ cup brown sugar
⅓ cup prepared spicy mustard

1. Place pork chops in slow cooker.

2. Mix remaining ingredients together in a bowl. Pour over chops.

3. Cover and cook on Low 6–8 hours, or until meat is tender but not dry.

Tropical Pork with Yams

Hope Comerford, Clinton Township, MI

Makes 6 servings

Prep. Time: 15 minutes ⚬ *Cooking Time: 7–8 hours* ⚬ *Ideal slow-cooker size: 5-qt.*

2–3-lb. pork loin

Salt and pepper, to taste

20-oz. can crushed pineapple

¼ cup honey

¼ cup brown sugar

¼ cup apple cider vinegar

1 tsp. low-sodium soy sauce

4 yams, peeled and cut into bite-sized chunks

1. Spray crock with nonstick spray.

2. Lay pork loin at the bottom of the crock, and salt and pepper it on both sides.

3. In a separate bowl, combine pineapple, honey, brown sugar, apple cider vinegar, and soy sauce. Mix together.

4. Place chunks of yams over and around the pork loin, and then pour pineapple sauce over the top.

5. Cover and cook on Low for 7–8 hours.

Lemon Dijon Fish

June S. Groff, Denver, PA

Makes 4 servings

Prep. Time: 10 minutes ⚬ *Cooking Time: 3 hours* ⚬ *Ideal slow-cooker size: 2-qt.*

1½ lbs. orange roughy fillets
2 Tbsp. Dijon mustard
3 Tbsp. butter, melted
1 tsp. Worcestershire sauce
1 Tbsp. lemon juice

1. Cut fillets to fit in slow cooker.

2. In a bowl, mix remaining ingredients together. Pour sauce over fish. (If you have to stack the fish, spoon a portion of the sauce over the first layer of fish before adding the second layer.)

3. Cover and cook on Low 3 hours, or until fish flakes easily but is not dry or overcooked.

Apricot Salsa Salmon

Sue Hamilton, Benson, AZ

Makes 2 servings

Prep. Time: 5 minutes ⚬ *Cooking Time: 1–1½ hours* ⚬ *Ideal slow-cooker size: 4-qt.*

12 ozs. frozen salmon fillets
(do not thaw)

¼ cup apricot jam

¼ cup roasted salsa verde

1. Grease interior of crock.

2. Place frozen salmon skin side down in bottom of cooker.

3. Mix together jam and salsa. Spread mixture over salmon.

4. Cover. Cook on Low for 1–1½ hours, or until an instant-read meat thermometer registers 135°F when stuck into center of fillet.

TIPS

1. Pass extra salsa to add to salmon while eating.

2. If you'd like to make your own salsa verde, here's a great recipe:

2 large oranges

¼ cup olive oil

¼ cup fresh lemon juice
(about 2 large lemons)

½ cup chopped fresh flat-leaf parsley

2 scallions, finely sliced

3 Tbsp. chopped fresh mint leaves

2 Tbsp. capers, rinsed and drained

2 Tbsp. orange zest

1 tsp. lemon zest

½–1 tsp. crushed red pepper flakes

Coarse salt and coarsely ground black pepper, *optional*

1. Peel oranges. Cut along the membrane on both sides of each segment and slide segments into medium bowl.

2. Stir in olive oil, lemon juice, parsley, scallions, mint, capers, orange zest, lemon zest, red pepper flakes and salt and pepper, if using.

3. Chop with immersion blender or in food processor.

Shrimp Marinara

Jan Mast, Lancaster, PA

Makes 4–5 servings
Prep. Time: 10–15 minutes ⚜ Cooking Time: 6¼–7¼ hours ⚜ Ideal slow-cooker size: 4-qt.

6-oz. can tomato paste

2 Tbsp. dried parsley

1 clove garlic, minced

¼ tsp. pepper

½ tsp. dried basil

1 tsp. dried oregano

Scant ½ tsp. salt

Scant ½ tsp. garlic salt

28-oz. can diced tomatoes, *divided*

1 lb. cooked shrimp, peeled

1. In slow cooker, combine tomato paste, parsley, garlic, pepper, basil, oregano, salt, garlic salt, and half the can of diced tomatoes.

2. Cook on Low 6–7 hours.

3. Turn to High and add shrimp.

4. If you'd like the sauce to have more tomatoes, stir in remaining tomatoes.

5. Cover and cook an additional 15–20 minutes.

Serving suggestion:

Serve over cooked spaghetti, garnished with grated Parmesan cheese if you wish.

Convenient Slow Cooker Lasagna

Rachel Yoder, Middlebury, IN

Makes 6–8 servings

Prep. Time: 30–45 minutes ❧ *Cooking Time: 4 hours* ❧ *Ideal slow-cooker size: 6-qt.*

1 lb. ground beef

29-oz. can tomato sauce

8-oz. pkg. lasagna noodles, uncooked, *divided*

4 cups shredded mozzarella cheese

1½ cups cottage cheese

1. Spray the interior of the cooker with nonstick spray.

2. Brown the ground beef in a large nonstick skillet. Drain off drippings.

3. Stir in tomato sauce. Mix well.

4. Spread one-fourth of the meat sauce on the bottom of the slow cooker.

5. Arrange ⅓ of the uncooked noodles over the sauce. If you wish, break them up so they fit better.

6. Combine the cheeses in a bowl. Spoon ⅓ of the cheeses over the noodles.

7. Repeat these layers twice.

8. Top with remaining meat sauce.

9. Cover and cook on Low 4 hours.

Turkey Lasagna

Hope Comerford, Clinton Township, MI

Makes 8 servings
Prep. Time: 30 minutes   ❧   Cooking Time: 3 hours   ❧   Ideal slow-cooker size: 6-qt.

1 lb. ground turkey

1 medium onion, chopped

Salt and pepper, to taste

28-oz. can crushed tomatoes

15-oz. can tomato sauce

2 tsp. Italian seasoning

1 tsp. garlic powder

1 tsp. onion powder

1 cup skim ricotta cheese

1½ cups shredded mozzarella cheese, *divided*

6–8 lasagna noodles, uncooked, *divided*

½ cup shredded Parmesan cheese

1. Spray crock well with nonstick spray.

2. Brown turkey with onion. Season with salt and pepper.

3. Add the crushed tomatoes, tomato sauce, Italian seasoning, garlic powder, and onion powder to the browned turkey/onion mixture and simmer on Low for about 5 minutes.

4. While the sauce is simmering, mix together the 1 cup ricotta cheese and 1 cup of the shredded mozzarella cheese. Set aside.

5. In the bottom of your crock, add ⅓ of the sauce.

6. Line the bottom of the crock with about 3 noodles.

7. Spread half of the ricotta/mozzarella mixture over the noodles and add ⅓ of the sauce again.

8. Add another layer of noodles, ricotta/mozzarella mixture, and remaining sauce.

9. Cook on Low for about 3 hours.

10. About 20 minutes before serving, sprinkle the top with remaining ½ cup mozzarella cheese and the Parmesan cheese.

Fresh Veggie Lasagna

Deanne Gingrich, Lancaster, PA

Makes 4–6 servings

Prep. Time: 30 minutes ⚜ Cooking Time: 4 hours ⚜ Ideal slow-cooker size: 4- to 5-qt.

1½ cups shredded mozzarella cheese

½ cup ricotta cheese

⅓ cup grated Parmesan cheese

1 egg, lightly beaten

1 tsp. dried oregano

¼ tsp. garlic powder

3 cups marinara sauce, *divided*, plus more for serving

1 medium zucchini, diced, *divided*

4 uncooked lasagna noodles, *divided*

4 cups fresh baby spinach, *divided*

1 cup fresh mushrooms, sliced, *divided*

1. Grease interior of slow-cooker crock.

2. In a bowl, mix together mozzarella, ricotta, Parmesan, egg, oregano, and garlic powder. Set aside.

3. Spread ½ cup marinara sauce in crock.

4. Sprinkle with half the zucchini.

5. Spoon ⅓ of cheese mixture over zucchini.

6. Break 2 noodles into large pieces to cover cheese layer.

7. Spread ½ cup marinara over noodles.

8. Top with half the spinach and then half the mushrooms.

9. Repeat layers, ending with cheese mixture and then sauce. Press layers down firmly.

10. Cover. Cook on Low 4 hours, or until vegetables are as tender as you like them and noodles are fully cooked.

11. Let stand 15 minutes so lasagna can firm up before serving.

Goulash

Janie Steele, Moore, OK

Makes 8-10 servings

Prep. Time: 15 minutes ♣ Cooking Time: 6 hours ♣ Ideal slow-cooker size: 5-qt.

1 lb. ground beef
1 pkg. taco seasoning
2 cups water
15-oz. can diced tomatoes
15-oz. can tomato sauce
15-oz. can whole-kernel corn, drained
Salt and pepper, to taste
2 cups uncooked elbow macaroni

1. Brown meat in a skillet and drain.

2. Mix remaining ingredients except the macaroni together and pour into slow cooker.

3. Add elbow macaroni, then mix.

4. Cover and cook 6 hours on Low.

Lasagna Casserole

Janie Steele, Moore, OK

Makes 8–10 servings
Prep. Time: 30 minutes ⚜ *Cooking Time: 6–7 hours* ⚜ *Ideal slow-cooker size: 5-qt.*

1 lb. ground beef

1 medium onion, chopped

4–5 cloves garlic, chopped

14-oz. can crushed tomatoes

24-oz. jar Prego Traditional Italian sauce

½ tsp. red pepper flakes (less if desired)

1 tsp. dried basil

1 tsp. dried parsley

1 tsp. dried oregano

1 dried bay leaf

Salt and pepper, to taste

16-oz. box lasagna noodles, broken into 1–2-inch pieces

Cheese garnish:

Shredded mozzarella

Grated Parmesan

Ricotta cheese

1. Brown ground beef, onion, and garlic in a skillet, then drain grease. Place in the crock.

2. Add the crushed tomatoes, Prego Traditional Italian sauce, and spices. Add lasagna noodles.

3. Cover and cook 6–7 hours on Low.

4. Garnish with all three cheeses, or use only what you desire.

Mexi Chicken Rotini

Jane Geigley, Lancaster, PA

Makes 6 servings
Prep. Time: 30 minutes ❧ *Cooking Time: 4 hours* ❧ *Ideal slow-cooker size: 4-qt.*

1 cup water or chicken broth

3 cups partially cooked rotini pasta

12-oz. pkg. frozen mixed vegetables

10-oz. can Ro*Tel diced tomatoes with green chilies

4-oz. can green chilies, undrained

4 cups cooked shredded chicken

1 cup shredded cheddar cheese

1. Combine all ingredients in slow cooker except shredded cheddar.

2. Cover and cook on Low for 4 hours.

3. Top with shredded cheddar, then let cook covered an additional 20 minutes or so, or until cheese is melted.

Gnocchi with Chicken

Janie Steele, Moore, OK

Makes 8 servings
Prep. Time: 30 minutes ⚜ Cooking Time: 7 hours ⚜ Ideal slow-cooker size: 5-qt.

1 lb. gnocchi, store-bought or homemade

2 cups cooked chicken, cut into cubes

1 onion, chopped

1 cup chopped or shredded carrots

2 cloves garlic

Salt and pepper, to taste

2 cups heavy cream

1½ cups grated Parmesan cheese

¼ tsp. nutmeg

1½ cups fresh chopped spinach

1. Cook gnocchi according to directions. Drain and add other ingredients to slow cooker except for spinach.

2. Cover and cook on Low for 7 hours. Add spinach during the last 30 minutes and serve.

Baked Ziti

Hope Comerford, Clinton Township, MI

Makes 8 servings
Prep. Time: 15 minutes & Cooking Time: 4 hours & Ideal slow-cooker size: 5-qt.

28-oz. can crushed tomatoes

15-oz. can tomato sauce

1½ tsp. Italian seasoning

1 tsp. garlic powder

1 tsp. onion powder

1 tsp. pepper

1 tsp. salt

1 lb. ziti or rigatoni pasta, uncooked, *divided*

1–2 cups shredded mozzarella cheese, *divided*

1. Spray crock with nonstick spray.

2. In a bowl, mix together crushed tomatoes, tomato sauce, Italian seasoning, garlic powder, onion powder, pepper, and salt.

3. In the bottom of the crock, pour ⅓ of the pasta sauce.

4. Add ½ of the pasta on top of the sauce.

5. Add another ⅓ of your pasta sauce.

6. Spread ½ of the mozzarella cheese on top of that.

7. Add the remaining pasta, the remaining sauce, and the remaining cheese on top of that.

8. Cover and cook on Low for 4 hours.

Tortellini with Broccoli

Susan Kasting, Jenks, OK

Makes 4 servings
Prep. Time: 10 minutes & *Cooking Time: 2½–3 hours* & *Ideal slow-cooker size: 4-qt.*

½ cup water

26-oz. jar pasta sauce

1 Tbsp. Italian seasoning

9-oz. pkg. frozen spinach and cheese tortellini

16-oz. pkg. frozen broccoli florets

1. In a bowl, mix water, pasta sauce, and seasoning together.

2. Pour ⅓ of sauce into bottom of slow cooker. Top with the tortellini.

3. Pour ⅓ of sauce over tortellini. Top with broccoli.

4. Pour remaining sauce over broccoli.

5. Cook on High 2½–3 hours, or until broccoli and pasta are tender but not mushy.

Slow Cooker Mac and Cheese

Jessica Stoner, Plain City, OH

Makes 4–6 servings

Prep. Time: 15–20 minutes ⚜ *Cooking Time: 3½ hours* ⚜ *Ideal slow-cooker size: 3-qt.*

4 cups cooked elbow macaroni
(1 cup dry)

2 eggs, beaten

1 cup shredded mild cheddar cheese

2 cups shredded sharp cheddar cheese

12-oz. can evaporated milk

½ cup milk

2 Tbsp. butter, melted, *optional*

1 tsp. salt

Pinch of pepper

1. Place cooked macaroni in slow cooker.

2. Mix all other ingredients in a separate bowl.

3. Pour over macaroni. *Don't stir!*

4. Cover and cook on Low for 3½ hours.

Mac & Cheese

Jolene Schrock, Millersburg, OH

Makes 8–10 servings
Prep. Time: 7 minutes ⚜ *Cooking Time: 2–3 hours* ⚜ *Ideal slow-cooker size: 5-qt.*

16 ozs. elbow macaroni
3 cups milk
8 ozs. Velveeta, cut into chunks
4 Tbsp. butter, cut into chunks
3 cups shredded cheddar cheese
¼ cup grated Parmesan cheese

1. Cook pasta in boiling water for 6 minutes.

2. Place the cooked macaroni, milk, Velveeta, butter, and cheddar cheese into a greased crock. Stir and top with Parmesan cheese.

3. Cover and cook on Low for 2–3 hours. Stir occasionally and check for doneness starting at the 2-hour mark.

Vegetarian Coconut Curry

Hope Comerford, Clinton Township, MI

Makes 10–14 servings
Prep. Time: 30 minutes ♣ Cooking Time: 4–5 hours ♣ Ideal slow-cooker size: 7-qt.

2 cups chopped broccoli

2 cups peeled and cubed butternut squash

1 cup chopped carrots

¾ cup chopped onion

¾ cup chopped celery

½ cup chopped mushrooms

15½-oz. can garbanzo beans, drained and rinsed

24-oz. container of Maya Kaimal Coconut Curry Sauce (or any other type of curry sauce you enjoy)

1. Place all the ingredients into the crock and stir.

2. Cover and cook on Low for 4–5 hours, or until vegetables are as tender as you like them.

Serving suggestion:

Serve this over cooked rice or pasta.

Vegetables and Red Quinoa Casserole

Gladys Voth, Hesston, KS

Makes 6–8 servings

Prep. Time: 20 minutes   ⚶   Cooking Time: 1½–4 hours   ⚶   Ideal slow-cooker size: 4-qt.

4 cups peeled and cubed butternut squash (¾-inch in size)

2 cups peeled and cubed beets (¾-inch in size)

2 cups sliced celery (½-inch thick), about 2 stalks

6 cloves garlic

1½ cups vegetable broth

3 Tbsp. dried basil

1 cup uncooked red quinoa, rinsed and drained

Mixed berry almond nondairy yogurt, for topping

½ cup cashews, for topping

1. Grease interior of crock.

2. Place butternut squash, beets, and celery in crock.

3. Coarsely chop garlic cloves. Place in crock.

4. Pour vegetable broth over ingredients in slow cooker.

5. Crush dried basil between your fingers while adding to slow cooker.

6. Stir everything together well.

7. Cover. Cook on High 1½–2 hours, or on Low 3–4 hours.

8. About 30 minutes before end of cooking time, stir in quinoa. Cover and cook on High 20–30 minutes.

9. Serve hot or at room temperature.

10. Top each serving with nondairy yogurt and a sprinkling of cashews.

Side Dishes & Vegetables

Honey-Orange Glazed Carrots

Hope Comerford, Clinton Township, MI

Makes 12 servings
Prep. Time: 5 minutes ☙ *Cooking Time: 8 hours* ☙ *Ideal slow-cooker size: 5-qt.*

3 lbs. baby carrots
2 Tbsp. freshly squeezed orange juice
½ cup honey
½ tsp. kosher salt
⅛ tsp. pepper
2 Tbsp. coconut oil
½ tsp. orange zest

1. Spray crock with nonstick spray.

2. Place carrots in crock, then add remaining ingredients except orange zest.

3. Cover and cook on Low for 8 hours.

4. Stir in orange zest before serving.

Steamed Carrots

Dede Peterson, Rapid City, SD

Makes 4 servings

Prep. Time: 15–20 minutes & *Cooking Time: 4–6 hours* & *Ideal slow-cooker size: 4-qt.*

8 large carrots, sliced diagonally

¼ cup water

2 Tbsp. butter, cut into pieces

1 tsp. sugar

¼ tsp. salt

1. Layer carrots in slow cooker. Add water and pieces of butter. Sprinkle with sugar and salt.

2. Cover and cook on Low 4–6 hours.

TIP
Stir in 1–2 Tbsp. brown sugar just before serving.

Slow Cooker Parmesan Ranch Mushrooms

Kris Zimmerman, Lititz, PA

Makes 6–8 servings

Prep. Time: 15 minutes & Cooking Time: 3–4 hours & Ideal slow-cooker size: 3-qt.

1 stick (8 Tbsp.) butter

2½ tsp. Hidden Valley ranch dressing mix

32 ozs. fresh mushrooms

2 tsp. Parmesan cheese

1. Melt butter in bowl in microwave.

2. Add ranch dressing mix to butter.

3. Place mushrooms in crock.

4. Pour butter mixture over mushrooms.

5. Sprinkle Parmesan cheese over mushrooms.

6. Cover and cook on Low 3–4 hours.

TIP
These mushrooms go great with grilled meat!

Wild Italian Mushrooms

Connie Johnson, Loudon, NH

Makes 4–5 servings

Prep. Time: 20 minutes   *Cooking Time: 6–8 hours*   *Ideal slow-cooker size: 5-qt.*

2 large onions, chopped

3 large red bell peppers, chopped

3 large green bell peppers, chopped

2–3 Tbsp. olive oil

12-oz. pkg. oyster mushrooms, chopped

4 cloves garlic, minced

3 fresh bay leaves

10 fresh basil leaves, chopped

1 Tbsp. salt

1½ tsp. pepper

28-oz. can Italian plum tomatoes, crushed or chopped

1. Sauté onions and peppers in oil in skillet until soft. Stir in mushrooms and garlic. Sauté just until mushrooms begin to turn brown. Pour into slow cooker.

2. Add remaining ingredients. Stir well.

3. Cover. Cook on Low 6–8 hours.

Mushrooms in Red Wine

Donna Lantgen, Chadron, NE

Makes 4 servings

Prep. Time: 10 minutes   ⚘   *Cooking Time: 4–6 hours*   ⚘   *Ideal slow-cooker size: 2-qt.*

1 lb. fresh mushrooms
4 cloves garlic, chopped
¼ cup chopped onion
1 Tbsp. olive oil
1 cup red wine

1. Combine all ingredients in slow cooker.

2. Cook on Low 4–6 hours, or until done to your liking.

Serving suggestion:

Serve with a sprinkle of grated Parmesan and as an accompaniment to your favorite meat.

Wine-Marinated Mushrooms

Hope Comerford, Clinton Township, MI

Makes 8–10 servings
Prep. Time: 5 minutes   ♣   Cooking Time: 6–8 hours   ♣   Ideal slow-cooker size: 3-qt.

4 lbs. mushrooms

1 Tbsp. Worcestershire sauce

3 cloves garlic, minced

4 Tbsp. butter

1 cup red wine

2 cups beef stock

1. Place mushrooms in crock with Worcestershire sauce, garlic, and butter. Pour the wine and stock over the top.

2. Cover and cook on Low for 6–8 hours.

Cheesy Creamed Corn

Michele Shenk, Manheim, PA

Makes 10–12 servings
Prep. Time: 15 minutes ❧ Cooking Time: 4 hours ❧ Ideal slow-cooker size: 3-qt.

3 pints corn
11 ozs. cream cheese, cubed
4 Tbsp. butter, cubed
6 slices American cheese
3 Tbsp. water
3 Tbsp. milk
2 Tbsp. sugar
2 tsp. salt
¼ tsp. pepper

1. Mix all ingredients well in slow cooker.

2. Cover and cook on Low for 4 hours.

TIP
This recipe may be doubled for larger crowds.

Chili Lime Corn on the Cob

Hope Comerford, Clinton Township, MI

Makes 6 servings
Prep. Time: 10 minutes ✿ Cooking Time: 4 hours ✿ Ideal slow-cooker size: 6-qt.

6 ears of corn, shucked and cleaned

6 Tbsp. butter, at room temperature

2 Tbsp. freshly squeezed lime juice

1 tsp. lime zest

2 tsp. chili powder

1 tsp. salt

½ tsp. pepper

1. Tear off 6 pieces of aluminum foil to fit each ear of corn. Place each ear of corn on a piece of foil.

2. Mix together butter, lime juice, lime zest, chili powder, salt, and pepper.

3. Divide butter mixture evenly between six ears of corn and spread it over ears of corn. Wrap them tightly with foil so they don't leak.

4. Place the foil-wrapped ears of corn into crock. Cover and cook on Low for 4 hours.

Very Special Spinach

Jeanette Oberholtzer, Manheim, PA

Makes 8 servings
Prep. Time: 10 minutes ☙ Cooking Time: 5 hours ☙ Ideal slow-cooker size: 4-qt.

3 10-oz. boxes frozen spinach, thawed and drained

2 cups cottage cheese

1½ cups grated cheddar cheese

3 eggs

¼ cup flour

1 tsp. salt

8 Tbsp. butter or margarine, melted

1. Mix together all ingredients.

2. Pour into slow cooker.

3. Cook on High 1 hour. Reduce heat to Low and cook 4 more hours.

Warm Eggplant and Kale Salad

Hope Comerford, Clinton Township, MI

Makes 8 servings
Prep. Time: 25 minutes ⚭ *Cooking Time: 4 hours* ⚭ *Ideal slow-cooker size: 4-qt.*

1-lb. eggplant, chopped

1 medium bunch kale, washed and coarsely chopped

1 yellow pepper, coarsely chopped

1 orange pepper, coarsely chopped

1 red onion, coarsely chopped

1 large zucchini, coarsely chopped

3 cloves garlic, minced

3 Tbsp. red wine vinegar

1 tsp. Dijon mustard

2 Tbsp. olive oil

½ tsp. sea salt

¼ tsp. pepper

1. Place all ingredients into crock and stir.

2. Cover and cook on Low for 4 hours.

Fresh Zucchini and Tomatoes

Pauline Morrison, St. Marys, ON

Makes 6–8 servings
Prep. Time: 15 minutes ⚘ Cooking Time: 2½–3 hours ⚘ Ideal slow-cooker size: 3½-qt.

1½ lbs. zucchini, peeled if you wish, and cut into ¼-inch slices

19-oz. can stewed tomatoes, broken up and undrained

1½ cloves garlic, minced

½ tsp. salt

1½ Tbsp. butter, cut into pieces

1. Place zucchini slices in slow cooker.

2. Add tomatoes, garlic, and salt. Mix well.

3. Dot surface with butter.

4. Cover and cook on High 2½–3 hours, or until zucchini is done to your liking.

Doris's Broccoli and Cauliflower with Cheese

Doris G. Herr, Manheim, PA

Makes 8 servings

Prep. Time: 5 minutes ☙ *Cooking Time: 1½–3 hours* ☙ *Ideal slow-cooker size: 3-qt.*

1 lb. frozen cauliflower, chopped

2 10-oz. pkgs. frozen broccoli, chopped

½ cup water

2 cups shredded cheddar cheese

1. Place cauliflower and broccoli in slow cooker.

2. Add water. Top with cheese.

3. Cook on Low 1½–3 hours, depending upon how crunchy or soft you want the vegetables.

Fresh Green Beans

Lizzie Ann Yoder, Hartville, OH

Makes 6-8 servings
Prep. Time: 20 minutes ❧ Cooking Time: 6-24 hours ❧ Ideal slow-cooker size: 4- to 5-qt.

¼ lb. ham or bacon pieces

2 lbs. fresh green beans, washed and cut into pieces or frenched

3-4 cups water

1 scant tsp. salt

1. If using bacon, cut it into squares and brown in nonstick skillet. When crispy, drain and set aside.

2. Place all ingredients in slow cooker. Mix together well.

3. Cover and cook on High 6-10 hours or on Low 10-24 hours, or until beans are done to your liking.

Roasted Butternut Squash

Marilyn Mowry, Irving, TX

Makes 15–20 servings
Prep. Time: 1 hour   ❧   Cooking Time: 4–6 hours   ❧   Ideal slow-cooker size: 6-qt.

¼ cup olive oil

2 tsp. cinnamon, *divided*

½ tsp. cumin

1¾ tsp. salt, *divided*

5-lb. butternut squash, split in quarters and seeds removed

2 carrots, diced

1 large white onion, diced

2 Granny Smith apples, peeled, cored, and quartered

1 can chipotle chilies in adobo, seeds scraped out and chopped roughly

10 cups chicken stock

1. Mix olive oil, 1 tsp. cinnamon, cumin, and ¾ tsp. salt in mixing bowl. Brush over the flesh of the quartered squash.

2. Place squash cut side down on a rimmed baking sheet lined with foil.

3. Add carrots, onion, and apples to bowl with oil and toss. Spread on another foil-lined sheet.

4. Roast both trays 40–50 minutes at 425°F until squash is soft and onion mixture is golden brown. Scoop out the squash.

5. Put squash, onion mixture, chipotle chilies, 1 tsp. salt, and 1 tsp. cinnamon in slow cooker. Add chicken broth.

6. Cover and cook on High 4 hours or Low for 6 hours. Mash with a potato masher or puree with immersion blender.

"Roasted" Vegetables

Hope Comerford, Clinton Township, MI

Makes 8 servings
Prep. Time: 15 minutes ⚜ Cooking Time: 6–7 hours ⚜ Ideal slow-cooker size: 5-qt.

2 large sweet potatoes, peeled and cut into cubes

1 large zucchini, coarsely chopped

1 large summer squash, coarsely chopped

2 red bell peppers, coarsely chopped

2 yellow bell peppers, coarsely chopped

1 large sweet yellow onion, coarsely chopped

1 tsp. sea salt

2 tsp. Italian seasoning

4 cloves garlic, chopped

4 Tbsp. olive oil or coconut oil

1. Place all vegetables into crock. Sprinkle with the sea salt, Italian seasoning, and garlic. Add oil. Stir to coat veggies well.

2. Cover and cook on Low for 6–7 hours.

Parmesan Potato Wedges

Carol and John Ambrose, McMinnville, OR

Makes 6 servings

Prep. Time: 15 minutes ❧ *Cooking Time: 4 hours* ❧ *Ideal slow-cooker size: 3-qt.*

2 lbs. red potatoes, cut into ½-inch wedges or strips

¼ cup chopped onion

2 Tbsp. butter, cut into pieces

1½ tsp. dried oregano

¼ cup grated Parmesan cheese

1. Layer potatoes, onion, butter, and oregano in slow cooker.

2. Cover and cook on High 4 hours, or until potatoes are tender but not dry or mushy.

3. Spoon into serving dish and sprinkle with cheese.

Lemon Red Potatoes

Carol Leaman, Lancaster, PA

Makes 6 servings

Prep. Time: 15–20 minutes ⚘ Cooking Time: 2½–3 hours ⚘ Ideal slow-cooker size: 3- to 4-qt.

10–12 small to medium red potatoes

¼ cup water

4 Tbsp. butter, melted

1 Tbsp. lemon juice

3 Tbsp. fresh or dried parsley

Salt and pepper, to taste

1. Cut a strip of peel from around the middle of each potato, using a potato peeler.

2. Place potatoes and water in slow cooker.

3. Cover and cook on High 2½–3 hours, or until tender. Do not overcook.

4. Drain water.

5. Combine butter, lemon juice, and parsley. Mix well. Pour over potatoes and toss to coat. Season with salt and pepper.

Best Smashed Potatoes

Colleen Heatwole, Burton, MI

Makes 12 servings

Prep. Time: 30 minutes & Cooking Time: 5–6 hours & Ideal slow-cooker size: 5½-qt.

5 lbs. potatoes, cooked, peeled, mashed, or riced

8 ozs. reduced-fat cream cheese, at room temperature

1½ cups reduced-fat sour cream, at room temperature

¾ tsp. garlic salt or onion salt

1½ tsp. salt

¼ tsp. pepper

2 Tbsp. butter, *optional*

1. Combine all ingredients in slow cooker.

2. Cover. Cook on Low 5–6 hours.

Irish Potato Balls

Jane Geigley, Lancaster, PA

Makes 6–8 servings

Prep. Time: 60 minutes ☙ *Cooking Time: 4–6 hours* ☙ *Ideal slow-cooker size: 6-qt.*

8 Tbsp. butter, *divided*

1 Tbsp. canola oil

½ cup chopped onion

½ cup chopped celery

4 cups mashed potatoes

4 cups cubed soft bread

4 eggs, beaten

1 tsp. salt

1 tsp. pepper

1. Melt 4 Tbsp. butter and oil in pan to fry onion and celery until golden.

2. Pour into slow cooker along with remaining ingredients except remaining 4 Tbsp. butter.

3. Form mixture into 1-inch balls.

4. Melt and pour remaining butter over balls and cook on Low for 4–6 hours.

German Potato Salad

Hope Comerford, Clinton Township, MI

Makes 6 servings
Prep. Time: 20 minutes ❧ Cooking Time: 5 hours ❧ Ideal slow-cooker size: 4-qt.

1 ½ lbs. red potatoes, coarsely chopped
1 medium onion, chopped
2 slices cooked bacon, chopped
1 cup chopped celery
¼ cup apple cider vinegar
2 Tbsp. whole-grain mustard
1 Tbsp. olive oil
½ tsp. sea salt
¼ tsp. pepper
1 Tbsp. cornstarch

1. Place potatoes, onion, bacon, and celery in crock.

2. In a small bowl, combine the apple cider vinegar, mustard, olive oil, salt, pepper, and cornstarch. Pour this over the contents of the crock and stir.

3. Cover and cook on Low for 5 hours or until potatoes are tender.

Ranch Hash Browns

Jean Butzer, Batavia, NY

Makes 5–6 servings

Prep. Time: 5 minutes   ✢   Cooking Time: 4–7 hours   ✢   Ideal slow-cooker size: 6-qt.

30-oz. bag frozen hash browns, partially thawed

8-oz. pkg. cream cheese, softened

1 envelope dry ranch dressing mix

10¾-oz. can cream of potato soup

1. Spray interior of slow cooker with nonstick spray.

2. Place potatoes in slow cooker. Break them up with a spoon if frozen together.

3. Mix remaining ingredients in a bowl. Stir gently into potatoes.

4. Cook on Low 4–7 hours, or until potatoes are cooked through. Stir carefully before serving.

Candied Sweet Potatoes

Julie Weaver, Reinholds, PA

Makes 8 servings
Prep. Time: 45 minutes ☙ Cooking Time: 4 hours ☙ Ideal slow-cooker size: 5-qt.

6–8 medium sweet potatoes

½ tsp. salt

4 Tbsp. butter or margarine, melted

20-oz. can crushed pineapple, undrained

¼ cup brown sugar

1 tsp. nutmeg

1 tsp. cinnamon

1. Cook sweet potatoes in boiling water until soft. Peel. Slice and place in slow cooker.

2. Combine remaining ingredients. Pour over sweet potatoes.

3. Cover. Cook on High 4 hours.

Cherry Wild Rice

Hope Comerford, Clinton Township, MI

Makes 6 servings
Prep. Time: 15 minutes ⚜ Cooking Time: 4–5 hours ⚜ Ideal slow-cooker size: 4-qt.

1½ cups uncooked wild rice
4 ozs. fresh sliced mushrooms
½ cup dried cherries
½ cup slivered almonds
3½ cups vegetable broth
1 Tbsp. coconut oil
½ tsp. salt
¼ tsp. pepper
3 cloves garlic, minced
3–4 green onions, sliced

1. Place all ingredients into your crock except the green onion. Stir to mix.

2. Cover and cook on Low for 4–5 hours.

3. Stir in the green onions just before serving.

Slow Cooker Rice

Jo Zimmerman, Lebanon, PA

Makes 16 servings
Prep. Time: 10 minutes ❧ *Cook Time: 2–3 hours* ❧ *Ideal slow-cooker size: 5½-qt.*

1 Tbsp. butter
4 cups partially cooked rice
10 cups water
1 tsp. salt

1. Grease crock with butter.

2. Pour rice, water, and salt into greased crock.

3. Cover and cook on High 2–3 hours.

TIP
To make the rice even more flavorful, substitute chicken stock for all or half of the water.

Basil Refried Beans

Jacqueline Swift, Perrysburg, NY

Makes 6–8 servings
Prep. Time: 20 minutes ⚜ *Cooking Time: 5–7 hours* ⚜ *Ideal slow-cooker size: 3-qt.*

2 Tbsp. butter

1 ½ cups diced onions

4 cups cooked pinto beans

½ cup vegetable broth

2 cloves garlic, minced

1 tsp. cumin

2 tsp. dried basil

½ tsp. dried rosemary

Pinch of cayenne pepper, or to taste

1 tsp. salt

½ cup shredded sharp cheddar cheese

1. Combine butter and onions in slow cooker.

2. Cover and cook on High for 1 hour.

3. Add beans, broth, garlic, cumin, basil, rosemary, cayenne pepper, and salt.

4. Cover and cook on Low for 4–6 hours.

5. Mash beans with potato masher. Stir in cheese until melted. Taste for seasoning before serving.

Desserts

Raspberry Lemon Cake

Hope Comerford, Clinton Township, MI

Makes 8 servings
Prep. Time: 10 minutes ☙ Cooking Time: 3½–4½ hours ☙ Ideal slow-cooker size: 3-qt.

3.9-oz. box lemon pudding mix

15¼-oz. box yellow cake mix, prepared according to box instructions

1 cup black or red raspberries

Powdered sugar, for dusting at serving

1. Spray crock with nonstick spray.

2. Stir the lemon pudding mix into the yellow cake batter.

3. Gently fold the raspberries into the cake mix/pudding mixture.

4. Pour this mixture into your crock. Cover and cook on Low for 3½–4½ hours with paper towel under the lid to catch the condensation.

5. Let the cake cool completely. Run a knife around the edge, then turn your crock upside down on a plate or platter. Dust the cake lightly with powdered sugar before serving if desired.

Zesty Orange Poke Cake

Hope Comerford, Clinton Township, MI

Makes 6–8 servings
Prep. Time: 10 minutes   Cooking Time: 6 hours   Ideal slow-cooker size: 3-qt.

Cake:

22-oz. box gluten-free yellow cake mix

½ cup freshly squeezed orange juice

½ cup water

⅓ cup melted coconut oil

3 eggs

1 Tbsp. orange zest

Glaze:

½ cup powdered sugar

1½ Tbsp. orange juice

1½ Tbsp. orange zest

Vanilla ice cream, *optional*

1. Spray crock with nonstick spray.

2. In a bowl, mix together all the cake ingredients. Pour into crock.

3. Cover and cook on Low for 6 hours.

4. Mix together the glaze ingredients.

5. With a straw, poke holes all over the cake. Pour the glaze over the top of the entire cake.

6. To serve, scoop the cake out of the crock with a spoon and top with vanilla ice cream if desired.

Gluten-Free Raspberry Dump Cake

Hope Comerford, Clinton Township, MI

Makes 12 servings

Prep. Time: 5 minutes ❧ Cooking Time: 4 hours ❧ Ideal slow-cooker size: 5-qt.

2 21-oz. cans raspberry pie filling

15–17-oz. box gluten-free yellow cake mix

1 stick (8 Tbsp.) butter, melted

1. Spray crock with nonstick spray.

2. Dump both cans of raspberry pie filling into crock and spread evenly.

3. Mix together the yellow cake mix with the butter, then spread evenly over the top of the raspberry pie filling.

4. Cover and cook on Low for 4 hours.

Chocolate Pudding Cake

Lee Ann Hazlett, Freeport, IL · Della Yoder, Kalona, IA

Makes 10–12 servings
Prep. Time: 5–10 minutes · Cooking Time: 3–7 hours · Ideal slow-cooker size: 4-qt.

18½-oz. box chocolate cake mix

3.9-oz. box instant chocolate pudding mix

2 cups sour cream

4 eggs

1 cup water

¾ cup vegetable oil

1 cup semisweet chocolate chips

1. Combine cake mix, pudding mix, sour cream, eggs, water, and oil in electric mixer bowl. Beat on medium speed for 2 minutes. Stir in chocolate chips.

2. Pour into a greased slow cooker. Cover and cook on Low 6–7 hours or on High 3–4 hours, or until a toothpick inserted near center comes out with moist crumbs.

Serving suggestion:
Top with whipped cream or ice cream if you wish.

Lotsa Chocolate Almond Cake

Hope Comerford, Clinton Township, MI

Makes 10 servings

Prep. Time: 10 minutes   Cooking Time: 3 hours   Cooling Time: 30 minutes   Ideal slow-cooker size: 6-qt.

1½ cups almond flour

¾ cup turbinado sugar

⅔ cup cocoa powder

¼ cup chocolate protein powder

2 tsp. baking powder

¼ tsp. salt

½ cup coconut oil, melted

4 eggs

¾ cup almond milk

1 tsp. vanilla extract

1 tsp. almond extract

¾ cup dark chocolate chips

1. Cover any hot spot of your crock with aluminum foil, and spray crock with nonstick spray.

2. In a bowl, mix together the almond flour, sugar, cocoa powder, protein powder, baking powder, and salt.

3. In a different bowl, mix together the coconut oil, eggs, almond milk, and vanilla and almond extracts.

4. Pour wet ingredients into dry ingredients and mix until well combined. Stir in chocolate chips.

5. Pour cake mix into crock. Cover and cook on Low for 3 hours.

6. Turn the slow cooker off when the cooking time is over and let the cake cool in the crock for 30 minutes.

7. Place a plate or platter over the crock, then turn the crock upside down on the plate, so the cake releases onto the plate or platter.

Peanut Butter and Hot Fudge Pudding Cake

Sara Wilson, Blairstown, MO

Makes 6 servings

Prep. Time: 10 minutes ☙ Cooking Time: 2–3 hours ☙ Ideal slow-cooker size: 4-qt.

½ cup flour

¾ cup sugar, *divided*

¾ tsp. baking powder

⅓ cup milk

1 Tbsp. vegetable oil

½ tsp. vanilla extract

¼ cup peanut butter

3 Tbsp. unsweetened cocoa powder

1 cup boiling water

1. Combine flour, ¼ cup sugar, and baking powder. Add milk, oil, and vanilla. Mix until smooth. Stir in peanut butter. Pour into slow cooker.

2. Mix together ½ cup sugar and cocoa powder. Gradually stir in boiling water. Pour mixture over batter in slow cooker. Do not stir.

3. Cover and cook on High 2–3 hours, or until a toothpick inserted comes out clean.

Serving suggestion:

Serve warm and with vanilla ice cream.

Seven Layer Bars

Mary W. Stauffer, Ephrata, PA

Makes 6–8 servings
Prep. Time: 5–10 minutes ⚹ Cooking Time: 2–3 hours ⚹ Ideal slow-cooker size: 4- to 5-qt.

¼ cup melted butter
½ cup graham cracker crumbs
½ cup chocolate chips
½ cup butterscotch chips
½ cup flaked coconut
½ cup chopped nuts
½ cup sweetened condensed milk

1. Layer ingredients in a bread or cake pan that fits in your slow cooker, in the order listed. Do not stir.

2. Cover and bake on High 2–3 hours, or until firm. Remove pan and uncover. Let stand 5 minutes.

3. Unmold carefully on plate and cool.

Zucchini Bars

Jane Geigley, Lancaster, PA

Makes 8 servings

Prep. Time: 30 minutes ⚘ *Cooking Time: 4–6 hours* ⚘ *Ideal slow-cooker size: 4-qt.*

Bars:

2 cups sugar

1 cup olive oil

4 eggs

2 cups flour

1 tsp. baking soda

1 tsp. baking powder

1 tsp. cinnamon

¼ tsp. salt

3 tsp. vanilla extract

½ tsp. nutmeg

2 cups shredded zucchini

Frosting:

2 cups confectioners' sugar

3 ozs. softened cream cheese

½ cup softened butter

1 tsp. milk

1 tsp. vanilla extract

1. Mix sugar and oil.

2. Beat in eggs.

3. Add the rest of bar ingredients except for the zucchini and blend until smooth.

4. Fold in zucchini.

5. Pour into greased slow cooker.

6. Cook on Low for 4–6 hours.

7. Prepare frosting by creaming sugar, cream cheese, and butter.

8. Beat in milk and vanilla.

9. Once bars are baked, pour frosting over them, cut, and serve warm.

Strawberry Rhubarb Crisp

Hope Comerford, Clinton Township, MI

Makes 6–8 servings
Prep. Time: 30 minutes ☙ Cooking Time: 2–3 hours ☙ Ideal slow-cooker size: 2½-qt.

Filling:

1 lb. strawberries, quartered if medium or large

3 rhubarb stalks, halved and sliced

½ cup sugar

2 Tbsp. flour

2 tsp. vanilla extract

Crisp:

⅓ cup sugar

2 Tbsp. flour

½ tsp. cinnamon

Pinch of salt

3 Tbsp. unsalted butter, cold and sliced

½ cup old-fashioned oats

2 Tbsp. chopped pecans

2 Tbsp. chopped almonds

1. Spray your crock with nonstick spray.

2. Place the strawberries and rhubarb into the crock.

3. In a bowl, mix together the sugar, flour, and vanilla. Pour this over the strawberries and rhubarb and stir to coat evenly.

4. In another bowl, start on the crisp. Mix together the sugar, flour, cinnamon, and salt. Cut the butter in with a pastry cutter.

5. Stir in the oats, pecans, and almonds. Pour this mixture over the contents of the crock.

6. Cover and cook on Low for 2–3 hours.

7. The last half hour of cooking, remove the lid to help the crisp thicken.

Serving suggestion:

Serve over vanilla ice cream or on yogurt.

Apple Caramel Pie

Sue Hamilton, Minooka, IL

Makes 8–10 servings
Prep. Time: 5 minutes ♣ Cooking Time: 3 hours ♣ Ideal slow-cooker size: 4- to 5-qt.

2-crust refrigerated pie dough pkg.
2 22-oz. cans apple pie filling
1 tsp. cinnamon
12 caramel candies

1. Press one crust into half the bottom of a cold slow cooker, and an inch or so up half its interior side. Overlap by ¼ inch the second crust with the first crust in center of slow cooker bottom. Press remainder of second crust an inch or so up the remaining side of the cooker. Press seams flat where two crusts meet.

2. Cover. Cook on High 1½ hours.

3. In a bowl, mix together pie filling, cinnamon, and caramels.

4. Pour mixture into hot crust.

5. Cover. Cook on High an additional 1½ hours.

Apple Crunch

Anita Troyer, Fairview, MI

Makes 6 servings
Prep. Time: 30 minutes & Cooking Time: 2½–3 hours & Ideal slow-cooker size: 6-qt.

Crumb:
1 cup flour
½ cup brown sugar
½ tsp. cinnamon
6 Tbsp. butter

Filling:
6 large Granny Smith apples
½ tsp. lemon juice
⅓ cup sugar
3 Tbsp. flour
½ tsp. cinnamon
⅛ tsp. nutmeg
⅛ tsp. salt

1. Spray crock very well with nonstick spray, or grease the inside of the crock very well with butter.

2. Mix all the crumb ingredients together. Set aside.

3. Peel, core, and cut the apples into ¼-inch slices.

4. In a bowl, mix the apples together with the other filling ingredients. Dump this mixture into the crock.

5. Place the crumb mixture over the top of the apple mixture in the crock.

6. Cover with a lid, placing a fork between lid and crock so that extra moisture can escape and crumbs will bake nicely. Cook on High for 2½–3 hours. Use care when removing the lid so that moisture on it will not drip on the crumbs.

Serving suggestion:
Serve with vanilla ice cream

Baked Apples

Marlene Weaver, Lititz, PA

Makes 4–6 servings
Prep. Time: 10 minutes ❧ *Cooking Time: 4 hours* ❧ *Ideal slow-cooker size: 6-qt.*

2 Tbsp. raisins
¼ cup sugar
6–8 baking apples, cored
1 tsp. cinnamon
2 Tbsp. butter
½ cup water

1. Mix raisins and sugar; fill center of apples.

2. Sprinkle with cinnamon and dot with butter.

3. Place in slow cooker; add water.

4. Cover and cook on Low for 4 hours.

Serving suggestion:
These apples are delicious with yogurt.

Apple Butter

Colleen Heatwole, Burton, MI

Makes 5–6 cups

Prep. Time: 45 minutes ❧ *Cooking Time: 22 hours* ❧ *Ideal slow-cooker size: 6- to 7-qt.*

12 lbs. apples, tart ones preferred, peeled, cored, and sliced

½ cup cider vinegar

1½ cups sugar

½ cup brown sugar

1 Tbsp. cinnamon

¼ tsp. ground cloves

1 tsp. allspice

1. Spray cooker with nonstick spray.

2. Combine apples and vinegar.

3. Place in large slow cooker. Cook on High 8 hours, then turn to Low and cook 10 hours more.

4. After 18 hours add spices and cook 4 hours more.

Serving suggestion:
Serve on buttered bread or on biscuits for breakfast.

Brown Rice Pudding

Colleen Heatwole, Burton, MI

Makes 6 servings
Prep. Time: 15 minutes ❧ Cooking Time: 4–6 hours ❧ Ideal slow-cooker size: 3-qt.

2½ cups cooked brown rice

1 cup evaporated milk

½ cup fat-free milk

3 eggs, beaten

½ cup raisins

½ cup brown sugar

2 Tbsp. butter, softened, plus a little more to butter slow cooker

½ tsp. cinnamon

½ tsp. salt

2 tsp. vanilla extract

1. Combine all ingredients thoroughly in mixing bowl.

2. Pour into buttered slow cooker.

3. Cover and cook on Low 4–6 hours, stirring once after the first hour.

4. Allow to cool to warm before serving.

Serving suggestion:

This dish is even better with a dollop of whipped cream and/or fresh fruit on top.

Buttery German Chocolate Fudge

Sue Hamilton, Benson, AZ

Makes 36 servings

Prep. Time: 15 minutes ⚜ *Cooking Time: 1–1½ hours* ⚜ *Ideal slow-cooker size: 6-qt.*

¼ cup water

20 Werther's Original caramel hard candies, unwrapped

15½-ounce container coconut pecan frosting

2 cups semisweet chocolate chips

4 ozs. (32, or one sleeve) round butter-type crackers, crushed (such as Ritz)

1. In a large slow cooker, put the water and the candies in a single layer. Try to place them where the water is sitting.

2. Cover and cook on Low for 1–1½ hours or until the candy is dissolved. If one or two pieces are left whole, remove them and stir well.

3. Add the frosting to the crock and stir until all the candy liquid is completely mixed in.

4. Sprinkle in the chocolate chips and mix until all the chocolate is melted.

5. Add the crushed crackers, stirring until coated.

6. Spread in a 9 x 9-inch or a 7 x 11-inch foil-lined pan that has been sprayed with nonstick spray.

7. Chill until firm.

8. Cut into 36 squares.

TIP
Crush the crackers in the sleeve in a ziplock bag.

Cherries Jubilee

Hope Comerford, Clinton Township, MI

Makes 4 servings
Prep. Time: 15 minutes & Cooking Time: 3–4 hours & Ideal slow-cooker size: 2-to- 3-qt.

1 lb. fresh cherries, pitted
½ cup turbinado sugar
1 tsp. lemon juice
1 tsp. lemon zest
1 tsp. vanilla extract
⅓ cup coconut rum
2 Tbsp. cornstarch
2 Tbsp. water
Vanilla ice cream, for serving

1. Spray crock with nonstick spray.

2. Place cherries in crock with turbinado sugar, lemon juice, lemon zest, vanilla, and coconut rum.

3. Mix together the cornstarch and water, then stir this mixture into the contents of the crock.

4. Cook on Low for 3–4 hours.

5. Serve over vanilla ice cream.

Hot Apricot Zinger

Jan Mast, Lancaster, PA

Makes 12 servings
Prep. Time: 10 minutes   ♣   Cooking Time: 2–4 hours   ♣   Ideal slow-cooker size: 4-qt.

46-oz. can apricot juice or nectar
3 cups orange juice
2 Tbsp. lemon juice
½ cup brown sugar
3 cinnamon sticks
½ tsp. whole cloves

1. Stir juices and brown sugar together in slow cooker.

2. Tie cinnamon sticks and cloves in a cheesecloth bag or coffee filter.

3. Add spice pack to juices.

4. Cook on Low 2–4 hours. Serve hot.

Spiced Apple Cider

Janice Muller, Derwood, MD

Makes 8–10 servings
Prep. Time: 20 minutes ☙ Cooking Time: 2–3 hours ☙ Ideal slow-cooker size: 6-qt.

2 sticks cinnamon

2 tsp. nutmeg

1 cup orange juice

1 tsp. whole cloves

1 tsp. cinnamon

½ cup pineapple juice

2 tsp. ground cloves

1 tsp. ginger

¼ cup lemon juice

1 tsp. lemon peel

3 tsp. whole allspice

1 gallon apple cider

1. Combine all the ingredients in slow cooker.

2. Cover and cook on Low 2–3 hours.

TIP

Place the crock in an easy-access point so that guests can serve themselves during the evening.

Christmas Caroling Chai

MarJanita Geigley, Lancaster, PA

Makes 6 servings
Prep. Time: 15 minutes ❧ Cooking Time: 2 hours ❧ Ideal slow-cooker size: 3-qt.

2½ cups water
2 Lipton tea bags (regular size)
1 cinnamon stick
¼ tsp. cardamom
1 whole clove
¼ tsp. ginger
3 cups warmed milk
½ cup sugar
Nutmeg, to taste, *optional*

1. Combine all ingredients in slow cooker except milk, sugar, and nutmeg.

2. Simmer on Low for 2 hours.

3. Strain.

4. Add milk, sugar, and nutmeg (if desired), and keep on Warm.

Serving suggestion:

Serve with chocolate-dipped spoons!

Sweet Country Tea

Jane Geigley, Lancaster, PA

Makes 12–16 servings
Prep. Time: 15 minutes ❧ *Cooking Time: 1 hour* ❧ *Ideal slow-cooker size: 5-qt.*

1 gallon water

2 handfuls of fresh Apple Meadow Tea or your favorite green or black tea leaves

½ cup sugar

1. Fill slow cooker with water.

2. Add tea leaves.

3. Steep on High for 1 hour.

4. Strain.

5. Add sugar (you can add more or less to taste) and stir.

6. Allow to cool to room temperature, then pour into glass jar.

7. Serve chilled.

Metric Equivalent Measurements

If you're accustomed to using metric measurements, I don't want you to be inconvenienced by the imperial measurements I use in this book.

Use this handy chart, too, to figure out the size of the slow cooker you'll need for each recipe.

Weight (Dry Ingredients)

1 oz		30 g
4 oz	¼ lb	120 g
8 oz	½ lb	240 g
12 oz	¾ lb	360 g
16 oz	1 lb	480 g
32 oz	2 lb	960 g

Slow-Cooker Sizes

1-quart	0.96 l
2-quart	1.92 l
3-quart	2.88 l
4-quart	3.84 l
5-quart	4.80 l
6-quart	5.76 l
7-quart	6.72 l
8-quart	7.68 l

Volume (Liquid Ingredients)

½ tsp.		2 ml
1 tsp.		5 ml
1 Tbsp.	½ fl oz	15 ml
2 Tbsp.	1 fl oz	30 ml
¼ cup	2 fl oz	60 ml
⅓ cup	3 fl oz	80 ml
½ cup	4 fl oz	120 ml
⅔ cup	5 fl oz	160 ml
¾ cup	6 fl oz	180 ml
1 cup	8 fl oz	240 ml
1 pt	16 fl oz	480 ml
1 qt	32 fl oz	960 ml

Length

¼ in	6 mm
½ in	13 mm
¾ in	19 mm
1 in	25 mm
6 in	15 cm
12 in	30 cm

Recipe and Ingredient Index

A
Allspice
Apple Butter, 305
Spiced Apple Cider, 315
Almond Date Oatmeal, 11
Almond milk
Apple Cinnamon Oatmeal, 15
Fresh Veggie and Herb Omelet, 25
"Hash Brown" Cauliflower Breakfast Bake, 33
Lotsa Chocolate Almond Cake, 289
Almonds
Cherry Wild Rice, 273
Strawberry Rhubarb Crisp, 297
Angie's Cheese Dip, 51
Any Bean, Any Burger Chili, 127
Apple Breakfast Risotto, 21
Apple Butter, 305
Apple Caramel Pie, 299
Apple cider
Cider and Pork Stew, 117
Cider Beef Stew, 113
Hot Spiced Cherry Cider, 89
Spiced Apple Cider, 315
Apple Cinnamon Oatmeal, 15
Apple Crunch, 301
Apples
Baked Apples, 303
Chunky Applesauce, 9
Cider Beef Stew, 113
Roasted Butternut Squash, 255
Applesauce
Apple-y Kielbasa, 77
Apple-y Kielbasa, 77
Apricot juice
Hot Apricot Zinger, 313
Apricot Salsa Salmon, 197
Apricot Stuffing and Chicken, 161
Arborio rice
Apple Breakfast Risotto, 21
Artichoke hearts
Garlicky Spinach and Artichoke Dip, 61
Roasted Pepper and Artichoke Spread, 59

B
Bacon
Bacon Cheddar Dip, 55
Fresh Green Beans, 253
German Potato Salad, 267
Kelly's Company Omelet, 27
Bacon Cheddar Dip, 55
Bacon drippings
Corn Chowder, 133
Bacon-Feta Stuffed Chicken, 159
Baked Apples, 303
Baked Ziti, 215
Barbecue sauce
Cranberry Chicken Barbecue, 143
Tangy Meatballs, 83
Barley
Chicken Barley Chili, 125
Basil
Any Bean, Any Burger Chili, 127
Bacon-Feta Stuffed Chicken, 159
Basil Refried Beans, 277
Fresh Tomato Soup, 95
Fresh Veggie and Herb Omelet, 25
Kelly's Company Omelet, 27
Lasagna Casserole, 209
Pesto Tomato Spread, 69
Shrimp Marinara, 199
Wild Italian Mushrooms, 235
Zucchini Quiche, 31
Basil Mint Tea, 87
Basil Refried Beans, 277
Beans
Any Bean, Any Burger Chili, 127
black
Chicken Barley Chili, 125
Chili Chicken Stew with Rice, 111
Summer Chili, 119
Taco Bean Soup, 107
chili
Summer Chili, 119
great northern
White Bean and Chicken Chili, 121

green
    Chicken and Vegetable Soup with Rice, 97
    Fresh Green Beans, 253
kidney
    Cabbage and Beef Soup, 105
    Chicken Chili, 123
    Taco Bean Soup, 107
navy
    White Bean and Chicken Chili, 121
pinto
    Taco Bean Soup, 107
refried
    Basil Refried Beans, 277
    Green Olive Bean Dip, 67
    Tostadas, 179
Beef
    Any Bean, Any Burger Chili, 127
    Cabbage and Beef Soup, 105
    Chili in a Slow Cooker, 129
    Cider Beef Stew, 113
    Convenient Slow Cooker Lasagna, 201
    Enchilada Casserole, 181
    Fajita Steak, 183
    Flavorful Pot Roast, 173
    Goulash, 207
    Green Chili Roast, 175
    Herby French Dip, 177
    Lasagna Casserole, 209
    Mexican Meatloaf, 185
    Nutritious Tasty Beef Stew, 115
    Onion Mushroom Pot Roast, 171
    Tostadas, 179
Beets
    Vegetables and Red Quinoa Casserole, 225
Bell pepper
    Any Bean, Any Burger Chili, 127
    Chicken Tortilla Soup, 101
    Chili in a Slow Cooker, 129
    Colorful Fruit Salsa, 73
    Fresh Veggie and Herb Omelet, 25
    Kelly's Company Omelet, 27
    Roasted Pepper and Artichoke Spread, 59
    "Roasted" Vegetables, 257
    Slim Dunk, 63
    Wild Italian Mushrooms, 235
    Zucchini Stew, 109
Best Smashed Potatoes, 263
Biscuits
    Caramel Rolls, 41

Slow Cooker Chicken and Dumplings, 155
Blueberry Fancy, 35
Bread
    Blueberry Fancy, 35
    Cheese Strata, 29
    Chicken and Dressing, 153
    French Toast, 37
    French Toast Casserole, 39
    Herby French Dip, 177
    Irish Potato Balls, 265
    Poppy Seed Tea Bread, 45
    Raspberry Chocolate Chip Bread, 47
Bread crumbs
    Chicken Parmigiana, 163
    Venetian Stuffed Mushrooms, 85
Breakfast Apples, 23
Broccoli
    Doris's Broccoli and Cauliflower with Cheese, 251
    Fresh Veggie and Herb Omelet, 25
    Tortellini with Broccoli, 217
    Vegetarian Coconut Curry, 223
Broccoli Cheese Soup, 93
Brown Rice Pudding, 307
Butterscotch chips
    Seven Layers Bars, 293
Buttery German Chocolate Fudge, 309

C
Cabbage and Beef Soup, 105
Cake mix
    Gluten-Free Raspberry Dump Cake, 285
    Raspberry Lemon Cake, 281
    Zesty Orange Poke Cake, 283
Candied Sweet Potatoes, 271
Caramel candies
    Apple Caramel Pie, 299
    Buttery German Chocolate Fudge, 309
Caramel Rolls, 41
Caramel sauce
    French Toast, 37
Cardamom
    Christmas Caroling Chai, 317
Carolina Pot Roast, 187
Carrot
    Chicken and Vegetable Soup with Rice, 97
    Chicken Tortilla Soup, 101
    Cider and Pork Stew, 117
    Cider Beef Stew, 113
    Fresh Tomato Soup, 95

Gnocchi with Chicken, 213
Honey-Orange Glazed Carrots, 229
Nutritious Tasty Beef Stew, 115
Roasted Butternut Squash, 255
Steamed Carrots, 231
Vegetarian Coconut Curry, 223
White Bean and Chicken Chili, 121

Cashews
Vegetables and Red Quinoa Casserole, 225

Cauliflower
Doris's Broccoli and Cauliflower with Cheese, 251
"Hash Brown" Cauliflower Breakfast Bake, 33

Cayenne
Basil Refried Beans, 277
Chili Chicken Stew with Rice, 111
French Onion Dip, 65
Kelly's Company Omelet, 27

Cheese
American
Cheesy Creamed Corn, 241
cheddar
Angie's Cheese Dip, 51
Bacon Cheddar Dip, 55
Basil Refried Beans, 277
Cheese Strata, 29
Chicken Tortilla Soup, 101
Doris's Broccoli and Cauliflower with Cheese,
251
"Hash Brown" Cauliflower Breakfast Bake,
33
Kelly's Company Omelet, 27
Mexican Meatloaf, 185
Mexi Chicken Rotini, 211
Slow Cooker Mac and Cheese, 219
Very Special Spinach, 245
cottage
Convenient Slow Cooker Lasagna, 201
Very Special Spinach, 245
cream
Bacon Cheddar Dip, 55
Best Smashed Potatoes, 263
Blueberry Fancy, 35
Cheesy Creamed Corn, 241
Crab Spread, 57
Creamy Italian Chicken, 151
Garlicky Spinach and Artichoke Dip, 61
Herbed Cheese Terrine, 71
Italiano Chicken, Rice, and Tomato Soup, 99
Lori's Two-Ingredient Cheese Sauce, 53

Pesto Tomato Spread, 69
Roasted Pepper and Artichoke Spread, 59
Zucchini Bars, 295
feta
Bacon-Feta Stuffed Chicken, 159
Fresh Veggie and Herb Omelet, 25
Herbed Cheese Terrine, 71
Mexican blend, 111
Enchilada Casserole, 181
mozzarella
Baked Ziti, 215
Convenient Slow Cooker Lasagna, 201
Easy Slow Cooker Italian Chicken, 141
Fresh Veggie Lasagna, 205
Garlicky Spinach and Artichoke Dip, 61
Green Olive Bean Dip, 67
Italiano Chicken, Rice, and Tomato Soup, 99
Lasagna Casserole, 209
Pesto Tomato Spread, 69
Turkey Lasagna, 203
Venetian Stuffed Mushrooms, 85
Parmesan
Chicken Parmigiana, 163
Fresh Veggie Lasagna, 205
Garlicky Spinach and Artichoke Dip, 61
Gnocchi with Chicken, 213
Lasagna Casserole, 209
Mac & Cheese, 221
Parmesan Potato Wedges, 259
Pesto Tomato Spread, 69
Roasted Pepper and Artichoke Spread, 59
Slow Cooker Parmesan Ranch Mushrooms,
233
Turkey Lasagna, 203
Zucchini Stew, 109
ricotta
Fresh Veggie Lasagna, 205
Lasagna Casserole, 209
Turkey Lasagna, 203
Velveeta, 93
Mac & Cheese, 221
Zucchini Quiche, 31
Cheese sauce
Angie's Cheese Dip, 51
Lori's Two-Ingredient Cheese Sauce, 53
Cheese soup
Broccoli Cheese Soup, 93
Cheese Strata, 29
Cheesy Creamed Corn, 241

Cherries
    Cherry Wild Rice, 273
Cherries Jubilee, 311
Cherry-flavored gelatin
    Hot Spiced Cherry Cider, 89
Cherry Wild Rice, 273
Chicken
    Apricot Stuffing and Chicken, 161
    Bacon-Feta Stuffed Chicken, 159
    Chili Chicken Stew with Rice, 111
    Cranberry Chicken Barbecue, 143
    Creamy Italian Chicken, 151
    Easy Slow Cooker Italian Chicken, 141
    Gnocchi with Chicken, 213
    Honey Baked Chicken, 157
    Italiano Chicken, Rice, and Tomato Soup, 99
    Mexi Chicken Rotini, 211
    Orange Garlic Chicken, 145
    Orange Glazed Chicken Breasts, 147
    Roast Chicken or Hen, 165
    Slow Cooker Chicken and Dumplings, 155
    White Bean and Chicken Chili, 121
Chicken and Dressing, 153
Chicken and Egg Noodle Dinner, 149
Chicken and Vegetable Soup with Rice, 97
Chicken Barley Chili, 125
Chicken Chili, 123
Chicken Parmigiana, 163
Chicken Tortilla Soup, 101
Chili
    Angie's Cheese Dip, 51
    Chicken Barley Chili, 125
    Chicken Chili, 123
    Lori's Two-Ingredient Cheese Sauce, 53
    Summer Chili, 119
    White Bean and Chicken Chili, 121
Chili Chicken Stew with Rice, 111
Chili in a Slow Cooker, 129
Chili Lime Corn on the Cob, 243
Chili powder
    Any Bean, Any Burger Chili, 127
    Chicken Barley Chili, 125
    Chicken Chili, 123
    Chili in a Slow Cooker, 129
Chipotle chilies
    Roasted Butternut Squash, 255
Chips
    Chicken Tortilla Soup, 101
    Colorful Fruit Salsa, 73

    Green Olive Bean Dip, 67
Chocolate chips
    Buttery German Chocolate Fudge, 309
    Chocolate Pudding Cake, 287
    Lotsa Chocolate Almond Cake, 289
    Raspberry Chocolate Chip Bread, 47
Chocolate Pudding Cake, 287
Christmas Caroling Chai, 317
Chunky Applesauce, 9
Cider
    v, 89
Cider and Pork Stew, 117
Cider Beef Stew, 113
Cinnamon
    Apple Butter, 305
    Apple Cinnamon Oatmeal, 15
    Apple Crunch, 301
    Baked Apples, 303
    Breakfast Apples, 23
    Brown Rice Pudding, 307
    Candied Sweet Potatoes, 271
    Caramel Rolls, 41
    Christmas Caroling Chai, 317
    Chunky Applesauce, 9
    French Toast, 37
    French Toast Casserole, 39
    Hot Apricot Zinger, 313
    Hot Spiced Cherry Cider, 89
    Maple-Glazed Turkey Breast with Rice, 167
    Raspberry Chocolate Chip Bread, 47
    Roasted Butternut Squash, 255
    Slow Cooker Maple and Brown Sugar
        Oatmeal, 19
    Spiced Apple Cider, 315
    Strawberry Rhubarb Crisp, 297
    Zucchini Bars, 295
Cinnamon rolls
    Custard Cinnamon Rolls, 43
Cloves
    Apple Breakfast Risotto, 21
    Apple Butter, 305
    Christmas Caroling Chai, 317
    Cranberry Pork Loin, 189
    Hot Apricot Zinger, 313
    Spiced Apple Cider, 315
Cocoa powder
    German Chocolate Oatmeal, 17
    Lotsa Chocolate Almond Cake, 289
    Peanut Butter and Hot Fudge Pudding Cake, 291

Coconut
    German Chocolate Oatmeal, 17
    Seven Layers Bars, 293
Coconut milk
    German Chocolate Oatmeal, 17
Colorful Fruit Salsa, 73
Convenient Slow Cooker Lasagna, 201
Coriander
    Chicken Tortilla Soup, 101
Corn
    Cheesy Creamed Corn, 241
    Chicken Barley Chili, 125
    Chili Chicken Stew with Rice, 111
    Chili Lime Corn on the Cob, 243
    cream-style
        Corn Chowder, 133
    Goulash, 207
    Taco Bean Soup, 107
    Turkey Rosemary Veggie Soup, 103
Corn Chowder, 133
Crabmeat
    Oceanside Bisque, 137
Crab Spread, 57
Crackers
    Buttery German Chocolate Fudge, 309
Craisins
    Slow Cooker Maple and Brown Sugar Oatmeal, 19
Cranberry Chicken Barbecue, 143
Cranberry Pork Loin, 189
Cream
    Chicken Tortilla Soup, 101
    Gnocchi with Chicken, 213
    Oceanside Bisque, 137
Cream cheese
    Bacon Cheddar Dip, 55
    Best Smashed Potatoes, 263
    Blueberry Fancy, 35
    Cheesy Creamed Corn, 241
    Crab Spread, 57
    Creamy Italian Chicken, 151
    Garlicky Spinach and Artichoke Dip, 61
    Herbed Cheese Terrine, 71
    Italiano Chicken, Rice, and Tomato Soup, 99
    Lori's Two-Ingredient Cheese Sauce, 53
    Pesto Tomato Spread, 69
    Roasted Pepper and Artichoke Spread, 59
    Zucchini Bars, 295
Cream of chicken soup
    Chicken and Egg Noodle Dinner, 149

Creamy Italian Chicken, 151
    Slow Cooker Chicken and Dumplings, 155
Cream of potato soup
    Ranch Hash Browns, 269
Cream-style corn
    Corn Chowder, 133
Creamy Italian Chicken, 151
Cumin
    Any Bean, Any Burger Chili, 127
    Basil Refried Beans, 277
    Chicken Barley Chili, 125
    Chicken Chili, 123
    Tostadas, 179
    White Bean and Chicken Chili, 121
Currant jelly
    Sausages in Wine, 79
Curry powder
    Honey Baked Chicken, 157
Curry sauce
    Vegetarian Coconut Curry, 223
Custard Cinnamon Rolls, 43

D
Dates
    Almond Date Oatmeal, 11
Doris's Broccoli and Cauliflower with
    Cheese, 251

E
Easy Slow Cooker Italian Chicken, 141
Egg noodles
    Chicken and Egg Noodle Dinner, 149
Eggplant
    Warm Eggplant and Kale Salad, 247
Eggs
    Blueberry Fancy, 35
    Chicken and Dressing, 153
    French Toast, 37
    French Toast Casserole, 39
    Fresh Veggie and Herb Omelet, 25
    Zucchini Quiche, 31
Enchilada Casserole, 181

F
Fajita Steak, 183
Fish
    Apricot Salsa Salmon, 197
    Lemon Dijon Fish, 195
Flavorful Pot Roast, 173

Flaxseed
    Slow Cooker Maple and Brown Sugar Oatmeal, 19
French Onion Dip, 65
French Toast, 37
French Toast Casserole, 39
Fresh Green Beans, 253
Fresh Tomato Soup, 95
Fresh Veggie and Herb Omelet, 25
Fresh Veggie Lasagna, 205
Fresh Zucchini and Tomatoes, 249

G
Garbanzo beans
    Vegetarian Coconut Curry, 223
Garlicky Spinach and Artichoke Dip, 61
Gelatin
    Hot Spiced Cherry Cider, 89
German Chocolate Oatmeal, 17
German Potato Salad, 267
Ginger
    Christmas Caroling Chai, 317
    v, 75
Gluten-Free Raspberry Dump Cake, 285
Gnocchi with Chicken, 213
Goulash, 207
Graham crackers
    Seven Layers Bars, 293
Granola
    Breakfast Apples, 23
Grape jelly
    Tangy Meatballs, 83
Grape Nuts
    Almond Date Oatmeal, 11
Gravy mix
    Flavorful Pot Roast, 173
Green beans
    Chicken and Vegetable Soup with Rice, 97
    Fresh Green Beans, 253
Green chilies
    Fajita Steak, 183
    Mexi Chicken Rotini, 211
    Summer Chili, 119
    Taco Bean Soup, 107
Green Chili Roast, 175
Green Olive Bean Dip, 67

H
Ham
    Fresh Green Beans, 253

Kale Chowder, 131
Kelly's Company Omelet, 27
"Hash Brown" Cauliflower Breakfast Bake, 33
Herbed Cheese Terrine, 71
Herby French Dip, 177
Honey Baked Chicken, 157
Honey-Orange Glazed Carrots, 229
Hot Apricot Zinger, 313
Hot sauce
    Cheese Strata, 29
    Fresh Veggie and Herb Omelet, 25
Hot Spiced Cherry Cider, 89

I
Ice cream
    Cherries Jubilee, 311
    Custard Cinnamon Rolls, 43
    Zesty Orange Poke Cake, 283
Irish Potato Balls, 265
Italian dressing
    Spicy Pork Chops, 191
Italian dressing mix
    Creamy Italian Chicken, 151
    Flavorful Pot Roast, 173
Italiano Chicken, Rice, and Tomato Soup, 99

J
Jalapeño
    Colorful Fruit Salsa, 73
    Orange Glazed Meatballs, 81
Jelly
    currant
        Sausages in Wine, 79
    grape
        Tangy Meatballs, 83

K
Kale
    Sausage and Kale Chowder, 135
    Warm Eggplant and Kale Salad, 247
Kale Chowder, 131
Kelly's Company Omelet, 27
Kielbasa
    Apple-y Kielbasa, 77

L
Lasagna
    Convenient Slow Cooker Lasagna, 201
    Fresh Veggie Lasagna, 205

Turkey Lasagna, 203
Lasagna Casserole, 209
Leek soup mix
    Slim Dunk, 63
Lemon Dijon Fish, 195
Lemon Red Potatoes, 261
Lori's Two-Ingredient Cheese Sauce, 53
Lotsa Chocolate Almond Cake, 289

M
Mac & Cheese, 219, 221
Maple-Glazed Turkey Breast with Rice, 167
Maple syrup
    Maple-Glazed Turkey Breast with Rice, 167
    Slow Cooker Maple and Brown Sugar Oatmeal, 19
Marjoram
    Orange Glazed Chicken Breasts, 147
Mayonnaise
    Crab Spread, 57
Meatballs
    Orange Glazed Meatballs, 81
    Tangy Meatballs, 83
Mexican Meatloaf, 185
Mexi Chicken Rotini, 211
Miracle Whip
    Slim Dunk, 63
Mushrooms
    Cherry Wild Rice, 273
    Creamy Italian Chicken, 151
    Fresh Veggie Lasagna, 205
    Onion Mushroom Pot Roast, 171
    Slow Cooker Parmesan Ranch Mushrooms, 233
    Vegetarian Coconut Curry, 223
    Venetian Stuffed Mushrooms, 85
    Wild Italian Mushrooms, 235
    Wine-Marinated Mushrooms, 239
Mushrooms in Red Wine, 237
Mustard
    Warm Eggplant and Kale Salad, 247

N
Noodles
    Chicken and Egg Noodle Dinner, 149
    Goulash, 207
Nutmeg
    Apple Breakfast Risotto, 21
    Apple Crunch, 301
    Candied Sweet Potatoes, 271
    Christmas Caroling Chai, 317

French Toast, 37
Gnocchi with Chicken, 213
Spiced Apple Cider, 315
Zucchini Bars, 295
Nutritious Tasty Beef Stew, 115

O
Oatmeal, instant
    Pineapple Baked Oatmeal, 13
Oats
    Almond Date Oatmeal, 11
    Apple Cinnamon Oatmeal, 15
    German Chocolate Oatmeal, 17
    Raspberry Chocolate Chip Bread, 47
    Slow Cooker Maple and Brown Sugar
        Oatmeal, 19
    Strawberry Rhubarb Crisp, 297
Oceanside Bisque, 137
Olives
    Green Olive Bean Dip, 67
    Herbed Cheese Terrine, 71
    Pesto Tomato Spread, 69
Onion Mushroom Pot Roast, 171
Onion soup mix
    Onion Mushroom Pot Roast, 171
Orange Garlic Chicken, 145
Orange Glazed Chicken Breasts, 147
Orange Glazed Meatballs, 81
Orange juice
    Honey-Orange Glazed Carrots, 229
    Hot Apricot Zinger, 313
    Spiced Apple Cider, 315
    Zesty Orange Poke Cake, 283
Orange marmalade, 81
Oranges
    Colorful Fruit Salsa, 73
Oregano
    Chicken Chili, 123
    Fresh Veggie Lasagna, 205
    Lasagna Casserole, 209
    Parmesan Potato Wedges, 259
    Shrimp Marinara, 199

P
Paprika
    Chicken and Vegetable Soup with Rice, 97
    Chicken Tortilla Soup, 101
    Italiano Chicken, Rice, and Tomato Soup, 99
Parmesan Potato Wedges, 259

Parsley
　　Turkey Rosemary Veggie Soup, 103
Pasta
　　Baked Ziti, 215
　　Chicken and Egg Noodle Dinner, 149
　　Convenient Slow Cooker Lasagna, 201
　　Easy Slow Cooker Italian Chicken, 141
　　Fresh Veggie Lasagna, 205
　　Goulash, 207
　　Lasagna Casserole, 209
　　Mac & Cheese, 221
　　Mexi Chicken Rotini, 211
　　Slow Cooker Mac and Cheese, 219
　　Tortellini with Broccoli, 217
　　Turkey Lasagna, 203
Peach Chutney, 75
Peaches
　　Colorful Fruit Salsa, 73
Peanut Butter and Hot Fudge Pudding Cake, 291
Pecans
　　French Toast, 37
　　French Toast Casserole, 39
　　Strawberry Rhubarb Crisp, 297
Peppermint
　　Basil Mint Tea, 87
Pesto Tomato Spread, 69
Pineapple
　　Candied Sweet Potatoes, 271
　　Colorful Fruit Salsa, 73
　　Tropical Pork with Yams, 193
Pineapple Baked Oatmeal, 13
Pineapple juice
　　Spiced Apple Cider, 315
Poppy Seed Tea Bread, 45
Pork
　　Carolina Pot Roast, 187
　　Cider and Pork Stew, 117
　　Cranberry Pork Loin, 189
　　Spicy Pork Chops, 191
　　Tropical Pork with Yams, 193
Potatoes. *See also* Sweet potatoes
　　Best Smashed Potatoes, 263
　　Carolina Pot Roast, 187
　　Cider and Pork Stew, 117
　　Cider Beef Stew, 113
　　Corn Chowder, 133
　　German Potato Salad, 267
　　Irish Potato Balls, 265
　　Kale Chowder, 131

　　Kelly's Company Omelet, 27
　　Lemon Red Potatoes, 261
　　Nutritious Tasty Beef Stew, 115
　　Parmesan Potato Wedges, 259
　　Ranch Hash Browns, 269
　　Turkey Rosemary Veggie Soup, 103
Pudding mix
　　Chocolate Pudding Cake, 287
　　Raspberry Lemon Cake, 281

Q
Quiche
　　Zucchini Quiche, 31
Quinoa
　　Vegetables and Red Quinoa Casserole, 225

R
Raisins
　　Baked Apples, 303
　　Brown Rice Pudding, 307
　　Peach Chutney, 75
　　Slow Cooker Maple and Brown Sugar Oatmeal, 19
Ranch dressing mix
　　Flavorful Pot Roast, 173
　　Ranch Hash Browns, 269
　　Slow Cooker Parmesan Ranch Mushrooms, 233
Ranch Hash Browns, 269
Raspberry Chocolate Chip Bread, 47
Raspberry Lemon Cake, 281
Raspberry pie filling
　　Gluten-Free Raspberry Dump Cake, 285
Red chilies
　　Peach Chutney, 75
Rhubarb
　　Strawberry Rhubarb Crisp, 297
Rice
　　Apple Breakfast Risotto, 21
　　Brown Rice Pudding, 307
　　Cherry Wild Rice, 273
　　Chicken and Vegetable Soup with Rice, 97
　　Chili Chicken Stew with Rice, 111
　　Italiano Chicken, Rice, and Tomato Soup, 99
　　Maple-Glazed Turkey Breast with Rice, 167
　　Slow Cooker Rice, 275
Ritz crackers
　　Buttery German Chocolate Fudge, 309
Roast Chicken or Hen, 165
Roasted Butternut Squash, 255
Roasted Pepper and Artichoke Spread, 59

"Roasted" Vegetables, 257
Rosemary
    Herby French Dip, 177
    Kelly's Company Omelet, 27
    Turkey Rosemary Veggie Soup, 103
Roughy
    Lemon Dijon Fish, 195
Rum
    Cherries Jubilee, 311

S
Sage
    Cider and Pork Stew, 117
Salmon
    Apricot Salsa Salmon, 197
Salsa
    Apricot Salsa Salmon, 197
    Colorful Fruit Salsa, 73
    Mexican Meatloaf, 185
    Nutritious Tasty Beef Stew, 115
Saltines
    Mexican Meatloaf, 185
Sausage
    Apple-y Kielbasa, 77
    "Hash Brown" Cauliflower Breakfast Bake, 33
    Kelly's Company Omelet, 27
    Zucchini Stew, 109
Sausage and Kale Chowder, 135
Sausages in Wine, 79
Seven Layers Bars, 293
Shallots
    Oceanside Bisque, 137
Sherry
    Oceanside Bisque, 137
Shrimp Marinara, 199
Slim Dunk, 63
Slow Cooker Chicken and Dumplings, 155
Slow Cooker Mac and Cheese, 219
Slow Cooker Maple and Brown Sugar
    Oatmeal, 19
Slow Cooker Parmesan Ranch Mushrooms, 233
Slow Cooker Rice, 275
Soup mix
    leek
        Slim Dunk, 63
Sour cream
    Best Smashed Potatoes, 263
    Chili Chicken Stew with Rice, 111
    Chocolate Pudding Cake, 287

Slim Dunk, 63
Soy sauce
    Herby French Dip, 177
    Tropical Pork with Yams, 193
Spearmint
    Basil Mint Tea, 87
Spiced Apple Cider, 315
Spicy Pork Chops, 191
Spinach
    Fresh Veggie Lasagna, 205
    Garlicky Spinach and Artichoke Dip, 61
    Gnocchi with Chicken, 213
    Slim Dunk, 63
    Tortellini with Broccoli, 217
    Very Special Spinach, 245
Squash
    Roasted Butternut Squash, 255
    "Roasted" Vegetables, 257
    Summer Chili, 119
    Vegetables and Red Quinoa Casserole, 225
    Vegetarian Coconut Curry, 223
Steamed Carrots, 231
Strawberry Rhubarb Crisp, 297
Stuffing mix
    Apricot Stuffing and Chicken, 161
Summer Chili, 119
Sun-dried tomatoes
    Herbed Cheese Terrine, 71
Sweet Country Tea, 319
Sweet potatoes. See also Yams
    Candied Sweet Potatoes, 271
    Cider and Pork Stew, 117
    "Roasted" Vegetables, 257

T
Taco Bean Soup, 107
Taco seasoning
    Mexican Meatloaf, 185
Tangy Meatballs, 83
Tapioca
    Nutritious Tasty Beef Stew, 115
Tarragon
    Kelly's Company Omelet, 27
Tea
    Basil Mint Tea, 87
    Christmas Caroling Chai, 317
    Sweet Country Tea, 319
Thyme
    Chicken and Dressing, 153

Cider and Pork Stew, 117
Cider Beef Stew, 113
Herby French Dip, 177
Kelly's Company Omelet, 27
Orange Garlic Chicken, 145
Tomatoes
    Any Bean, Any Burger Chili, 127
    Bacon-Feta Stuffed Chicken, 159
    Baked Ziti, 215
    Cabbage and Beef Soup, 105
    Chicken Barley Chili, 125
    Chicken Chili, 123
    Chicken Tortilla Soup, 101
    Chili in a Slow Cooker, 129
    Enchilada Casserole, 181
    Fajita Steak, 183
    Fresh Tomato Soup, 95
    Fresh Veggie and Herb Omelet, 25
    Fresh Zucchini and Tomatoes, 249
    Goulash, 207
    Lasagna Casserole, 209
    Mexi Chicken Rotini, 211
    Pesto Tomato Spread, 69
    Shrimp Marinara, 199
    Summer Chili, 119
    sun-dried
        Herbed Cheese Terrine, 71
    Taco Bean Soup, 107
    Turkey Lasagna, 203
    White Bean and Chicken Chili, 121
    Wild Italian Mushrooms, 235
    Zucchini Stew, 109
Tomato sauce
    Baked Ziti, 215
    Chicken Parmigiana, 163
    Convenient Slow Cooker Lasagna, 201
    Easy Slow Cooker Italian Chicken, 141
    Fajita Steak, 183
    Fresh Veggie Lasagna, 205
    Goulash, 207
    Lasagna Casserole, 209
    Tortellini with Broccoli, 217
Tortellini with Broccoli, 217
Tortilla chips
    Chicken Tortilla Soup, 101
    Colorful Fruit Salsa, 73
    Green Olive Bean Dip, 67
Tortillas
    Enchilada Casserole, 181

Tostadas, 179
Traditional Turkey Breast, 169
Tropical Pork with Yams, 193
Turkey
    Chicken Barley Chili, 125
    Maple-Glazed Turkey Breast with Rice, 167
    Traditional Turkey Breast, 169
    Turkey Lasagna, 203
Turkey Lasagna, 203
Turkey Rosemary Veggie Soup, 103

V
V8 juice
    Chili in a Slow Cooker, 129
Vegetables and Red Quinoa Casserole, 225
Vegetarian Coconut Curry, 223
Velveeta
    Broccoli Cheese Soup, 93
    Mac & Cheese, 221
Venetian Stuffed Mushrooms, 85
Very Special Spinach, 245
Vinegar
    apple cider
        Apple Butter, 305
        German Potato Salad, 267
        Tropical Pork with Yams, 193
    balsamic
        Orange Garlic Chicken, 145
    Cider Beef Stew, 113
    red wine
        Warm Eggplant and Kale Salad, 247

W
Warm Eggplant and Kale Salad, 247
White Bean and Chicken Chili, 121
Wild Italian Mushrooms, 235
Wild rice
    Cherry Wild Rice, 273
Wine
    Mushrooms in Red Wine, 237
    Sausages in Wine, 79
Wine-Marinated Mushrooms, 239

Y
Yams. *See also* Sweet potatoes
    Tropical Pork with Yams, 193
Yogurt
    French Onion Dip, 65
    Garlicky Spinach and Artichoke Dip, 61

Herbed Cheese Terrine, 71
Vegetables and Red Quinoa Casserole, 225

Z
Zesty Orange Poke Cake, 283
Zucchini
    Fresh Veggie Lasagna, 205

Fresh Zucchini and Tomatoes, 249
"Roasted" Vegetables, 257
Summer Chili, 119
Warm Eggplant and Kale Salad, 247
Zucchini Bars, 295
Zucchini Quiche, 31
Zucchini Stew, 109

About the Author

Hope Comerford is a mom, wife, elementary music teacher, blogger, recipe developer, public speaker, FitAddict Training fit leader, Young Living Essential Oils essential oil enthusiast/ educator, and published author. In 2013, she was diagnosed with a severe gluten intolerance and since then has spent many hours creating easy, practical, and delicious gluten-free recipes that can be enjoyed by both those who are affected by gluten and those who are not.

Growing up, Hope spent many hours in the kitchen with her Meme (grandmother), and her love for cooking grew from there. While working on her master's degree when her daughter was young, Hope turned to her slow cookers for some salvation and sanity. It was from there she began truly experimenting with recipes and quickly learned she had the ability to get a little more creative in the kitchen and develop her own recipes.

In 2010, Hope started her blog, "A Busy Mom's Slow Cooker Adventures," to simply share the recipes she was making with her family and friends. She never imagined people all over the world would begin visiting her page and sharing her recipes with others as well. In 2013, Hope self-published her first cookbook, *Slow Cooker Recipes: 10 Ingredients or Less and Gluten-Free*, and then later wrote *The Gluten-Free Slow Cooker*.

Hope became the new brand ambassador and author of Fix-It and Forget-It in mid-2016. She is excited to bring her creativity to the Fix-It and Forget-It brand. Through Fix-It and Forget-It, she has written *Fix-It and Forget-It Lazy & Slow* as well as *Fix-It and Forget-It Healthy Slow Cooker Cookbook*.

Hope lives in the city of Clinton Township, Michigan, near Metro Detroit. She's a native of Michigan and has lived there her whole life. She has been happily married to her husband and best friend, Justin, since 2008. Together they have two children, Ella and Gavin, who are her motivation, inspiration, and heart. In her spare time, Hope enjoys traveling, singing, cooking, reading books, spending time with friends and family, and relaxing.

FIX-IT and FORGET-IT®